DELIVERING ON THE PROMISE OF DEMOCRACY

DELIVERING ON THE PROMISE OF DEMOCRACY

Visual Case Studies in Educational Equity and Transformation

Sukhwant Jhaj

https://www.openbookpublishers.com

© 2019 Sukhwant Jhaj

This work is licensed under a Creative Commons Attribution 4.0 International license (CC BY 4.0). This license allows you to share, copy, distribute and transmit the text; to adapt the text and to make commercial use of the text providing attribution is made to the authors (but not in any way that suggests that they endorse you or your use of the work). Attribution should include the following information:

Sukhwant Jhaj, *Delivering on the Promise of Democracy. Visual Case Studies in Educational Equity and Transformation.* Cambridge, UK: Open Book Publishers, 2019. https://doi.org/10.11647/OBP.0157

In order to access detailed and updated information on the license, please visit https://www.openbookpublishers.com/product/856#copyright

Further details about CC BY licenses are available at https://creativecommons.org/licenses/by/4.0/

All external links were active at the time of publication unless otherwise stated and have been archived via the Internet Archive Wayback Machine at https://archive.org/web

Updated digital material and resources associated with this volume are available at https://www.openbookpublishers.com/product/856#resources

Publication of *Delivering on the Promise of Democracy, Visual Case Studies in Educational Equity and Transformation* was made possible by a grant from the Bill & Melinda Gates Foundation.

This is the seventh volume of our Open Report Series

ISSN (print): 2399-6668
ISSN (digital): 2399-6676

ISBN Paperback: 978-1-78374-595-1
ISBN Hardback: 978-1-78374-596-8
ISBN Digital (PDF): 978-1-78374-597-5
ISBN Digital ebook (epub): 978-1-78374-598-2
ISBN Digital ebook (mobi): 978-1-78374-599-9
ISBN Digital (XML): 978-1-78374-692-7
DOI: 10.11647/OBP.0157

The interior of this book has been designed by XPLANE, www.xplane.com

All paper used by Open Book Publishers is SFI (Sustainable Forestry Initiative), PEFC (Programme for the Endorsement of Forest Certification Schemes) and Forest Stewardship Council® (FSC® certified).

Printed in the United Kingdom, United States, and Australia by Lightning Source for Open Book Publishers (Cambridge, UK)

CONTENTS

Acknowledgments ix

Forward 1
Jeffrey J. Selingo

Introduction 2

Florida International University 6
    Interview with Mark B. Rosenberg 10
    Florida International University Visual Case Study 14

Johnson C. Smith University 16
    Interview with Ronald L. Carter 20
    Johnson C. Smith University Visual Case Study 24

National Louis University 26
    Interview with Nivine Megahed 30
    National Louis University Visual Case Study 34

Georgia State University 36
    Interview with Mark P. Becker 40
    Georgia State University Visual Case Study 44

Delaware State University 46
    Interview with Harry L. Williams 50
    Delaware State University Visual Case Study 54

Mercy College 56
    Interview with Tim Hall 60
    Mercy College Visual Case Study 64

Portland State University 66
    Interview with Wim Wiewel 70
    Portland State University Visual Case Study 74

To my parents,
Didar Jhaj and Yashwant Jhaj,
thank you for your faith in me.

ACKNOWLEDGMENTS

I express my thanks to all those who contributed to this book with their ideas, time, resources, and patience. In particular, I thank Nina Narella and Tim May from XPLANE for being my creative partners on this adventure, Suzzane Walsh from Bill & Melinda Gates Foundation for funding this exploration, and Lori Coulter and Christopher Knaus for coordinating this project. I am indebted to Mark P. Becker, Roald L. Carter, Tim Hall, Nivine Megahed, Mark B. Rosenberg, Wim Wiewel, and Harry L. Williams who took time out to their busy schedule to share their thoughts on leadership and institutional transformation. Also, I thank my colleagues from multiple institutions who shared their work, including Aarti Dhupelia and Diane Trausch from National Louis University; Mike Boone, Lisa Dunning, Teresa Hardee, and Georgeann Hawyard from Delaware State University; Isis Artze-Vega, Sat Becerra, Elizabeth Bejar, Laird Kramer, Leanne Wells, Damaris Valdes from Florida International University; Ben Brandon, Allison Calhoun-Brown, Carol Cohen, Tim Renick, Ben Welling, Ethel Brown from Georgia State University; Helen Caldwell, Antonio Henley, Brian Jones, Laura McLean, and Sherri Belfield from Johnson C. Smith University; Jessica Haber, Jose Herrera, Raj Kumar, Tori Mondelli, Joan Toglias, Grace Creighton from Mercy College; Sona Karentz Andrews, Cindy Baccar, Johannes De Gruyter, Randi Harris, Hans VanDerSchaaf, Nicole Bannon, and Brian Rozendal from Portland State University; Megan Donaldson, Ryan Brown, Sara Messing, Kirse May, Amy Martin, and Nicole Bittner from XPLANE, and Shannon Looney from USU/APLU Office of Urban Initiatives. Thanks also to Alessandra Tosi and the staff at Open Book Publishers. Finally, I thank my family for their patience and encouragement: Jasjeet, Baaz, Joesh, Amrit, and Ranger.

FORWARD

Twenty-one years ago, I started on a journey of writing about colleges and universities as a young reporter at the *Chronicle of Higher Education*. I never set out to be a "higher-education writer," nor did I ever think in 1997 that I'd still be writing about the topic to this day. But what I discovered in those first few years at the *Chronicle* is that higher education is the gateway to the American dream, and that as a result, colleges and universities are critical not only to education, but to the economy, to citizenship, and to society.

Yet we all know too well the flaws of that higher-education system: too few students are graduating from college, too many are leaving with too much debt, and there is a growing economic divide among the haves and have nots, with both students and institutions. In the last few years, the focus of my research and writing has centered almost exclusively on how we can improve the higher education system through innovative practices and approaches to build a future that is going to look much different than the recent past.

I have traveled the country spending time with students, faculty members, and administrators on campuses of all kinds and sizes to figure out what makes institutions tick, who drives innovation, and what the barriers to change are. What I found is that while new ideas to transform teaching, financial aid, and student services often bubble up from experiments in the trenches, it is institutional leaders that encourage innovation by setting the tone, crafting the narrative for internal and external constituencies, and finding the money to expand boutique projects.

As the pages that follow in this book will outline, I have found that transformation isn't a formula from a box that can be easily replicated from campus to campus. A change of mindset is needed at the top if leaders are to embrace innovation to create institutions focused on their students' future. In the decades ahead, it is my belief that prestige in higher education will be measured by those institutions that focus on expanding access to the neediest students, improve completion of all students, and help graduates find their passions in life.

The future of work, indeed the future of our country, depends on our higher-education system thinking differently about how to prepare the next generation of talent. It will require leaders who ask the right questions, who are willing to experiment (and fail), and who are prepared to attempt new approaches to problem solving. This book provides an excellent starting point for leaders in higher education as they begin on that journey.

Jeffrey J. Selingo
Author, Columnist, and Founding Director of the Arizona State/Georgetown University Academy for Innovative Higher Education Leadership

INTRODUCTION
by Sukhwant Jhaj
Portland, Oregon

THE GENESIS OF THE PROJECT

The inspiration for this project came from a retreat sponsored by the Bill & Melinda Gates Foundation for the Frontier Set, a select group of colleges and universities, state systems, and supporting organizations committed to significantly increasing student access and success and eliminating racial/ethnic and socioeconomic disparities in college attainment. This convening of university presidents and chancellors took place in March 2016 in Phoenix, Arizona, where I joined the president of Portland State University to brainstorm with others about solving large-scale problems in higher education.

In July 2016, the Bill & Melinda Gates Foundation funded my proposal to develop "visual case studies" to highlight institutions and their approaches, with the hope that insights into their successes would be valuable for anyone interested in the evolving story of higher education. I invited seven leaders from the Frontier Set to participate in our research so we could highlight their unique leadership, processes, and institutional strategies. I partnered with XPLANE, a Portland, Oregon based design consultancy firm which specializes in design thinking and cooperative facilitation, to facilitate the field research and develop this visual case study.

My desire to lead this research was driven by the belief that higher education institutions, as we have conceptualized them, are neglecting key segments of society. The accepted best practices for student success are not reaching many students who could most benefit from access to the ladder of education. I have always understood that the mission of higher education is to provide such access for the improvement of the communities these institutions serve.

This belief is connected to my own journey. My father first sought education as a young man of 14 at a village school in India, literally under a tree. His educational journey expanded his possibilities and in turn opened a world of opportunity to me. In my role as a faculty member and academic leader, I am acutely aware of what happens to students and their families—and future generations—once they partake in education, study, and complete their degrees. The students and their families follow a different trajectory. As an architect, I believe that form must always follow function. Institutions likewise must ask the question: is our form following our mission, our institutional function and purpose?

I chose these seven institutions as exemplars in improving access, increasing graduation rates, building innovative programmes, designing advising and student support services to facilitate greater student success, and using technology to improve learning. I interviewed the institutions' executives to explore how they approached problems for their specific institutions and how they lead transformation.

METHODOLOGY

I traveled to each institution, interviewing executive leaders and asking them a series of questions about their path to leadership, challenges faced by their institutions, their leadership style, their approach to ideas like innovation and change, and how they understood and communicated a vision for their institution. These interviews have been transcribed and edited for inclusion in each case study.

In addition to president and executive interviews, we also facilitated group discovery sessions with project leaders from each campus, with the design team at XPLANE videoconferencing to visually document these discussions. Using design methodologies in our discovery sessions, the groups were able to quickly convey the essence of their work. The result of these sessions are illustrated in the visual case studies.

WHAT WE DISCOVERED

Leaders who managed to transform their institutions did not begin with a detailed road map. They began with questions that allowed them to shift perspectives and move things forward. A common defining moment among these institutions was when these leaders reframed their problems as opportunities, reflecting the mantra of Marcus Aurelius: 'The impediment to action advances action. What stands in the way becomes the way'. They walked toward the challenge and found that in the obstacles lay the path forward. They changed the point of view—the barrier is the way.

These leaders were also conscientious about approaching questions of institutional transformation as questions of values. How do we serve all students? How do we approach disparities? Emerging from these studies was the importance of cultural framing, the vision around which people can rally and which motivates change and provides clarity. In each case the institution's needs and the leader's approach were symbiotic: leaders' personal journeys informed their leadership style, which aligned with problems faced by their institutions.

We did not discover, however, a set of solutions to be universally replicated. Each institution has its own unique history and challenges and therefore its own unique solutions. We uncovered a process of igniting transformation that was common to all the institutions, and we believe this approach to problem-solving can be applied to various schools regardless of their disparate challenges.

Spark

Every leader interviewed faced some kind of major challenge when they joined their institution, whether it was a budget crisis, changing political agendas, or a mandate to better serve their students. Regardless of their specific issues, these leaders reframed their challenge as a spark of opportunity to advance their institution's mission.

Sense-Making

To better understand issues facing their institutions, leaders listened to those around them. In some cases, that meant meeting with students, faculty, and staff to better understand their challenges; in other cases, it meant involving the community in creating a shared vision for their school. Successful leaders guided these discussions and helped define the focus.

New Vision

For some schools, the new vision that emerged represented a new direction for the institution, such as centering the student experience or using student data in innovative ways. For others, it was a matter of refining their vision to better align their services with students' needs.

Team/Mandate

To realize their new shared vision, departments and teams were empowered with a high degree of autonomy and decision-making authority. Leaders limited their school's focus to a few projects at a time, encouraging collaboration and delegating responsibilities across the institution.

Iteration

As employees witnessed successes across their organization, they were emboldened to take more risks toward improvement and to acknowledge and learn from mistakes, leading to even more successes and a sustainable culture of innovation.

THE POWER OF DESIGN AND VISUAL CASE STUDY

We used design methods, techniques, and habits of minds of designers because we wanted to demonstrate the value of design practice beyond the common design context of architecture or product design. In the creation of visual case studies, we used key design practices: user centered approach, problem framing, visualization, experimentation, and prototyping. We believe a designerly approach can reduce ambiguity when discussing large scale change projects.

The design problem facing higher education is the simultaneous action of making existing functions of an organization more effective while seeking disruptive innovation for long term success. A parallel exists between institutional effort (working on two opposing ideas simultaneously, i.e. focusing on both short- and long-term goals) and the kind of exploration that is central to design. Designers, and design theory and practice, can play a role similar to that played by social science researchers and social science over the past three decades–to design solutions to higher education problems: initiatives, curriculum, support services, learning space, and the design of the organization itself. In the postsecondary setting, where most employees who engage in change initiatives are non-designers, they can benefit from the application of design theory, concepts, and techniques to better understand problems and create solutions. Many of the institutions profiled found unity through a type of design: getting a plan and vision on paper. The agreements and conversations necessary to produce that document can be a key step in designing the future.

I hope these case studies will serve as a call to action. If we are to deliver on the promise of democracy in the United States and beyond, it will require deep and sustained transformation of the educational institutions in this country. Through the case studies that follow, we discover that clarity of purpose, for both public and private institutions, can be transformative, and institutions must transform themselves to serve all citizens. We also hope to inspire readers with the evidence that when the purpose becomes clear—although the path might be strenuous—and you build community around the challenge and work together to design new solutions, it is a joyous undertaking.

FLORIDA INTERNATIONAL UNIVERSITY
Miami, Florida

Florida International University (FIU) significantly improved student success by implementing major educational reforms in its Science, Technology, Engineering and Mathematics (STEM) and gateway courses while launching a series of university-wide innovations in the areas of advising and support through their *Graduation Success Initiative*. This effort resulted in improved passing and graduation rates across all courses. The six-year graduation rate for first-time-in-college (FTIC) students at FIU increased 15 points in the first four years.

FIU's *Graduation Success Initiative* is a comprehensive, university-wide system of innovations that introduced a professional advisor model, adding 74 advisor lines (considerably lowering the student-to-advisor ratio), and provided students with several electronic tools. Crucial to this initiative was the *My eAdvisor Student Dashboard*, which allows students and advisors to monitor academic progress. These interventions help students identify a major, provide a clear path to on-time graduation, remove barriers, and add support.

Core elements of these initiatives are interventions that

1. Adapt evidence-based instructional practices to the FIU context
2. Require engaged active learning by students in the classroom
3. Are initiated by external grant or foundation funding
4. Integrate undergraduates, faculty, and multiple administrative units.

'I realized when I became president […] I was going to philosophically reframe my efforts around an optimistic, forward-facing, unapologetic framework […] a thought process that was not cursing the darkness, not benchmarking against the past, but trying to look into the future and […] figure out how to utilize our demography and our geography as assets rather than liabilities. […] We don't want to measure ourselves by who we exclude. We want to measure ourselves by who's included and how well they do and what we can do with them'.

– President Mark B. Rosenberg

MARK B. ROSENBERG
President of Florida International University

Mark B. Rosenberg earned a BA in 1971 from Miami University of Ohio and a PhD in 1976 in Political Science with a focus on Latin America from the University of Pittsburgh. Rosenberg began teaching at FIU in 1979. As provost and executive vice president for Academic Affairs, he played a significant role in the growth and expansion of FIU as a major public research university in the region. He was the first FIU faculty member to become university president, serving as its fifth president since 2009.

In many ways FIU is the demographic future, and Rosenberg has been instrumental in guiding his institution forward. During his tenure, student enrollment has increased along with the addition of over 500 new faculty, accompanied by a focus on improving graduation and retention. FIU leads the country in granting minority degrees in science and engineering and has developed trailblazing partnerships with schools and businesses of Miami.

Interview with

MARK B. ROSENBERG

This Interview Has Been Edited and Condensed for Clarity

How has your personal journey informed your motivations to do this work?

I was raised in a university community, but my father was a businessman in town, so I was raised around the sons and daughters of university professors. A lot of my formative years were spent in a university environment. However, I never thought that I would be a professor, much less a university president.

Fast forward to being an undergraduate at Miami University of Ohio. I got a great liberal arts education surrounded by deep-thinking faculty, and the further I got into my undergraduate education, the more windows in my mind were opened by these faculty. The academic life began to call. I thought I'd be a lawyer, but I didn't like the pre-law courses. I found myself heavily influenced by a number of faculty members who encouraged me to go to graduate school. I chose to study Latin America. I was very interested in poverty because I was raised in one of the poorest counties in Ohio, Athens County. There was so much poverty around me, I wanted to understand its political causes and consequences. The University of Pittsburgh—I got an excellent education there at a very difficult time. The Vietnam War was winding down and there were very few job opportunities when I graduated. I was lucky to get a job. There were four hundred applicants for the political science position at FIU.

I liked the idea of FIU because having been raised in a community in one of the old public universities, the history of that university was basically written. I could come to a new public university and the history had yet to be built. And a new university where nobody could tell you, 'We don't do things that way'. It was only four years old when I started. Latin America … in Miami. What a great opportunity. You mean I could actually get a job in a place where we used to take vacations, get paid for it, and be in the closest Latin American city to Latin America, namely Miami? It was perfect. I thought I'd died and gone to heaven, and truthfully I feel that same way 41 years later.

We've built this university, and the thing that's carried me through is the students and their determination to succeed. This is a community which has the highest generation of foreign-born people, right here in Miami. I identify with that because my mom was an immigrant.

She was a survivor of Auschwitz. She was liberated by my dad, whose parents were immigrants. He was born in the States and he was an army officer, came across at Normandy, but he was an officer of all black troops. So it's an interesting juxtaposition, coming from my family, then coming here to a community where so many people had been displaced or were immigrants. I aligned with that.

What does *innovation* mean to you in the context of your work as an institutional leader?

Innovation needs to pivot around our context and our ability to see into the future. Vision is the art of seeing the impossible. What does the future look like? How must we adapt? What do we need to maintain from an institutional perspective? In a mainstream North American university context, what do we need to change to get to where we need to go? We're lucky at FIU because we don't have a lot of traditions. In the olden days, that would have been a deficit. Today, it's probably an asset.

How did you experience the severity of external pressures on your institution?

So much of what we do is routinized and institutionalized and formulaic that it's easy to stay in traditional channels. I realized when I became president that I had to make a choice. It was a choice I hadn't been willing to make prior to becoming president, but I knew that I had to figure out how to make sure that the glass was always at least half-full. Given the route that we followed to build this university, given the context, the wider context of so much difficulty, so much pain, so much uncertainty, so much negativity, I made a choice that I was going to philosophically reframe my efforts around an optimistic, forward-facing, unapologetic framework.

The university being so new, a lot of us, including me, used to curse the darkness. That is to say that we dreamed about being able to have graduate students. We dreamed about being able to have residence halls. We dreamed about being able to become a research university with serious research labs and a major library with two million volumes. It was essentially a deficit thinking, always trying to figure out how to fill the gaps between who we were and who we wanted to be.

In the process of trying to think through how I would provide leadership and work with people and be optimistic about that, I realized I needed a thought process that was not cursing the darkness, not benchmarking against the past, but trying to look into the future and understand where we needed to go, what we needed to do, and how we were going to get there. And more importantly, to figure out how to utilize our demography and our geography as assets rather than liabilities.

Ours was a demography of recent arrivals, immigrants, people in exile, people carrying around identities that were inconsistent with traditional notions of Americana and traditional notions of assimilation. As we began to think through who we were and where we were, and as we began to embrace a more forward-facing logic, we realized our geography could be an asset. Our demography most certainly is an asset, because we are where America's going in terms of demography. Today we're 72% Hispanic, 14% African diaspora. What an asset to have that different kind of outlook, everybody brought together with an exile, immigrant, get-up-and-go, let's-get-things-done attitude.

The major drivers have varied across time. I do think that demographics and the geography, they are the context. Anybody who forgets those drivers is not going to survive here long. You have significant boom/bust cycles that affect Florida and Miami, as a consequence of the sharp connections we have here. We're a global city and a global community, so we reflect those dynamics. We're sitting on the edge, driven by different global and international factors.

Within the state we are getting a thousand new people a day, this overall population pressure. We don't have this sunset mentality, this 'What do we have to do today to get to the next day?' in terms of meeting people's needs.

We also have more recently had a powerful entrepreneurial input. Entrepreneurship is taking off in this community. Some of those are traditional mom-and-pop operations as a consequence of immigration and the nature of it, but some of it is creatives who want to be in Miami, and they find what's going on in Miami conducive to their innovation and entrepreneurial instincts.

Interview with Mark P. Rosenberg

So we've had demographic inputs, we've had financial economic inputs, we've had creative inputs. We also have a huge digital divide. We also have huge income inequality. So we have issues that we have to address.

State support is up and down, so anybody who thinks they can build a responsive institution dependent upon state support in this era is not going to get much done. I don't pay much attention to student/faculty ratios anymore. I want to know what our students learn, that's what I want to know. And that's where we need to be in the twenty-first century.

How would you describe the leadership structure you created?

Structure is less important than mindset and leadership. I'm pretty eclectic as it relates to structure. I'll look at what works. I don't have an instinctive knee-jerk reaction to talent per se. I like to work with people where they are and get them to the next level if possible. I like to work with people who are competitive; that's very important. I like to work with people who take risks. I like to work with people who will challenge authority, but who will also be good team players when necessary.

I like information; I don't like vertical relationships. The best relationships are horizontal, and people need to talk with each other and communicate with each other. Having said that, I meet regularly with all the vice presidents and sometimes we get into operations. I try to leave the operations to them, but since I know so much about this university and I've been raised here, I will tell people, 'Listen, you may think this is micromanagement, but really this is just curiosity'. I helped build the programme, I know the people, I dreamed the dream to create the thing because I have been privileged to be here for so long, which is perhaps a disadvantage.

I have these operating rules that help manage the tensions between the urgent, the important, the short-term, and the long-term. Number one: The key to success is a mastery of routine. Number two: You build from that base. Everybody wants a tree with a lot of branches, but if you don't have a strong trunk, the tree will fall over. Number three: You're always stressed by the contradiction between being and becoming, and what's urgent will always replace what's important. Then the final:

In terms of working with my team and mentoring, I always challenge myself with the question, 'Do I want to be right or do I want to be effective?'.

I prefer sins of commission rather than omission. Omission drives me crazy because we have a responsibility to get better every day and to learn from our mistakes, and to be unapologetic for pointing out where somebody could do better. I expect people to do that with me, too.

How did you frame your vision for this work? What was the story you told about why this was important?

Plans are important, but planning isn't everything. I do believe in planning, I do believe in preparing. We've made a lot of mistakes, but we've also gotten a lot done because we've had a lot of risk-takers. We've done pretty good in setting a plan, but we've never been rigid.

I use my bully pulpit a lot to talk about change, how important it is, and to make sure that we're in the process of creating change, not reacting to it. For higher education in the next decade and a half, that will be determinative. We are in the service industry in the end. You have to get better and better at offering those services, because particularly for us, in our domain, students have choices now. In the old days, they didn't have choices.

We don't want to measure ourselves by who we exclude. We want to measure ourselves by who's included and how well they do and what we can do with them. We see ourselves as a "solution center". We see ourselves taking responsibility for our community. My point is that we have the blessings of talent here, and we need to put that talent to work to solve problems. I'm pretty explicit in talking in those terms.

We don't feel we can turn our backs on our community. And we can't curse the darkness, because if you think about it, 35% of the teachers in Miami Dade County are FIU graduates. So if we're not happy with the quality of students we get from K-12, we have nobody to blame but ourselves. In other words, we take responsibility and figure out how to address the problem.

We know in the end that we have something special in universities because people identify in important ways with their universities. We are very good at building an experience that has value both in and out of the classroom. You should work toward having a place that symbolizes the aspiration, a place that is hospitable and safe and responsive. But we can't get overextended. We're not going to be all things to all people. But the organizational philosophy should be that if we can be, we should be. If we can be, then we can do it well.

Florida International University Visual Case Study

Sense-Making

FIU knew it could not rely on traditional university models, which were not designed to serve students on the margins; traditional methods would continue to exacerbate inequality. Improving student success would require classroom impact, evidence-based experimentation, and a focus on teaching and instructional design.

Spark

In 2007–2008 FIU faced a budget crisis which required downsizing and closing programmes. University leadership took this challenge as an opportunity to strategize about how to rebuild when funds became available. This crisis catalyzed the university to become clearer about its goals, decision-making process, and use of data and evidence.

New Vision

The bold new vision for the university paralleled the vision it had always held for its students. The leadership wanted to ensure the university could emerge from the margins, experience financial stability, and act as a community leader. To that end, the university determined to become the research institution of the future through its unique identity as an urban university with over 50% first-generation students and nearly 80% minority student population.

Executive Leadership

As a prior faculty member, President Mark B. Rosenberg inspires a compelling emotional narrative about the importance of inclusion, the necessity of removing barriers to student success, and the value of teaching and learning. He understood that people closest to students—and the students themselves—were the experts on supporting student success.

Team/Mandate

The pathway was not always linear or mandated from the top, but rather a coalescing and focusing of initiatives across the organization. Central to the process of innovation and experimentation was an organizational culture open to new ideas and to failure, and to learning quickly to adjust.

Iteration

'You have to want to make an impact. You have to want to roll up your sleeves and work. We are about infrastructure and building and continuously improving. We're always focusing on *it's never good enough*, but I like to look at it as *we can do better*. We can build, we can build, we can build'.

Florida International University Graduation Success Initiative

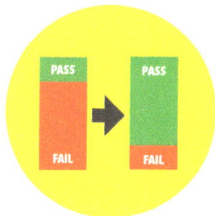

GRADUATION SUCCESS INITIATIVE (GSI)

Core elements of the GSI programme include helping students identify a major early-on, delineating clear paths to on-time graduation, and providing additional supports.

PROFESSIONAL ADVISING

Students receive high-touch, professional advising in conjunction with digital advising dashboard and tools.

MODIFIED MASTERY FOR GATEWAY COURSES

High-tech labs and high-touch teaching assistants provide extra support for critical "gateway" courses in STEM, resulting in a pass/fail reversal from 30/70 to 70/30 in College Algebra.

CENTER FOR THE ADVANCEMENT OF TEACHING (CAT) AND STEM TRANSFORMATION INSTITUTE

Many of the programmatic innovations began in physics, with results so promising that the CAT and STEM Transformation Institute scaled them throughout STEM and core curriculum.

LEARNING ASSISTANT (LA) PROGRAMME

Undergraduate students build skills as facilitators in the classroom, contributing their cultural competency and content expertise and supporting other students in their learning success.

Who They Serve

The majority of FIU's students come from historically underserved backgrounds, including over 50% first-generation students and nearly 80% minorities.

Providing Access

FIU provides multiple pathways for admission with varying standards depending on the programme. Some students are admitted directly into a four-year graduation track, some through partnerships with a local community college, some through a more supported and stepped entry.

Enabling Success

By providing comprehensive student support services and by maintaining an optimistic and forward-leaning view of possibilities for both itself as an institution and its students as future leaders, FIU ensures greater student and community success.

JOHNSON C. SMITH UNIVERSITY
Charlotte, North Carolina

The University College provides a comprehensive experience designed to connect first-year students to the institution, preparing students for university life and beyond. In doing so, the college strives to develop students' communication, ability to reason, leadership, and career skills. The college operates three interrelated divisions: the First-Year Experience, the Biddle Institute, and Liberal Studies.

The First-Year Experience supports students' transition to the university and the enrichment of their academic skills. It coordinates orientation and retention programmes, academic support services, and professional development programmes. It also manages the Hub, an academic support center that houses the Academic Center for Excellence Advising, Student Support Services, Math Lab, and the Writing Studio.

The Biddle Institute innovatively offers research and direct student services. Using strengths-based assessments, it investigates and provides academic support to students admitted to the university. Students are given "strengths awareness trainings" and are connected with in-classroom learning and out-of-class experiences. These trainings result in structured support programming through faculty teaming and intrusive advising as well as co-curricular excursions, academic success workshops, and community service activities. They also provide a greater institutional understanding of the extent to which grit, perseverance, or motivation can predict college success.

Liberal Studies delivers the core curriculum of the general education. It strengthens students' competencies as critical thinkers, capable writers, and cogent speakers. Courses also promote student development as life-long learners and global leaders. This division manages the academic experience for all students who are undecided about a major degree programme of study.

'Why do we do what we do? For what good purpose? […] Is it to screen out those I perceive not contributing to quality? […] Or do I need to rethink the very meaning of quality, so that it's inclusive and it's diverse? […] Education is not meant to screen; it is meant to include. And for what purpose? To use John Silber's words, to "maintain the promise of democracy".

– President Ronald L. Carter

RONALD L. CARTER
President of Johnson C. Smith University
Years of Service: 2008–2017

Ronald L. Carter graduated Phi Beta Kappa from Morehouse College with a BA in Sociology and Philosophy in 1971, then earned a Master of Theology degree and a PhD in Philosophy of Religion from Boston University. In the 1980s he moved to South Africa to work at University of the North, then becoming dean of students at a historically white institution, the University of the Witwatersrand in Johannesburg. He returned to the United States in 1997 as the provost and dean of faculty at Coker College in Hartsville, South Carolina. He became the thirteenth president of JCSU on 1 July 2008 and served until 31 December 2017.

Under his leadership, the mission of JCSU expanded to focus on the future of the institution, concentrating on the demographic shifts and challenges facing higher education. His team increased the university's majors, expanded academic offerings, and developed new and innovative programmes to support student success. With robust fundraising campaigns, an increased endowment, and the university's investments in the Charlotte community, JCSU has become a model of an independent urban university.

Interview with

RONALD L. CARTER

This Interview Has Been Edited and Condensed for Clarity

How has your personal journey informed your motivations to do this work?

I have always been in higher education. From the time I enrolled at Morehouse College to my first job at Boston University, where I was—and don't laugh, the janitor, but a janitor in higher education—I always felt, 'This is where I can envision myself: in higher education'. I found emotional strength. I found emotional security. I learned how to network. I progressed from being a graduate student, working as a cleaner, to becoming a mentor in the Martin Luther King, Jr. Center for African-American Studies at Boston University, then becoming assistant director in the Center, then becoming director, then becoming dean of students at the university.

The way people live and learn at their "growing edge" is to always have a vision of themselves they can summon. To be able to be patient with themselves, but persistent. To have the emotional strength to hang tough with that vision, and to look for ways to be comfortable with that vision, and then to take advantage of networking. That's fabulous, to be able to seek people and opportunities and co-create realities around that. This is the way one thrives. That's my journey in higher education and why I'm still in higher education.

I learned how to be a passionate "change agent" in South Africa. Throughout my life, I knew I wanted to change things, but I couldn't figure out, 'How do I articulate it?'. In South Africa I found the language, the force of the language, the "gripping language" for radical transformation. One of my tasks was to bring together with an official from the United States (who was part of USAID) the seven national student leaders who had been tasked by the exile parent bodies to overthrow de Klerk's government. We were told, 'You will never make it happen', because these young people had been fighting each other; they were at odds with each other. We came up with a scenario to make it happen, but it required working with each group separately for over a year, listening to the values that prompted them, that sustained them, that kept them persistent—though impatient. We created a "gripping language" that we thought they all could speak. I'll never forget the day they all agreed to come to a meeting, to see them sitting around a table saying, 'Okay, we're going to put our differences aside and look at why we are doing what we are doing, for what purpose'. We kept that in front of them, and they emerged as a group to do what needed to be done. All that prepared me for what I'm doing here at Smith.

That is a defining characteristic of a "change agent". You have to be patient and persistent when you're most alone. You never lose sight of the vision. That was the beginning of being able to talk to these student leaders because they said, 'We know that you're not here to just kick the dust'. That's the statement they had about foreigners who came into South Africa: They were kicking dust to make money. I was there because I believed they were going to be the future of South Africa, and I had a commitment to doing what I could to help.

What does *innovation* mean to you in the context of your work as an institutional leader?

I use the words of Adam Kahane, in the book *Solving Tough Problems*: we have a commitment to co-creating new realities around natural processes. The symbolic thinking in co-creating new realities is summed up in *innovation*, that we have an inward journey around what we see as possible. It taps into the good purpose for why we want to see things progress. We want to ameliorate, if you will, things that keep us from living and learning at our "growing edge". So, the more we define the purpose, and the more we see how this purpose can lead to progress, we see something that comes together in a new way. We say this is an innovation, something that now can be communicated in a way that leads to progress on common ground.

Innovation is a social-relational concept. You may see something; I may see something. We get together and we start asking, 'What if?'. That involves what Adam Kahane calls "scenario planning". We don't say to each other, 'That's silly, that's not going to work'. We just keep saying, 'What if? What if?'. If you carry this responsibility of innovation at your university, you will wrestle with your own thinking. But at certain points, you get up from your desk and you say to somebody, 'I have this idea. I want to engage you with it'. That engagement is what gives substance. So we live as co-creators.

How did you experience the severity of external pressures on your institution?

The board of trustees in 2008 when I came aboard, I describe as a group of futurists. They were asking what kind of institution should Johnson C. Smith University be in 2020, in 2025. As they were raising that question, Chronicle Research Services came out with 'The College of 2020: Students,'[3] which said that by 2020, the majority of students attending colleges and universities will come from minority groups. For the first time in contemporary American history, the white American student would be in the minority. The board saw this and said, 'If that is the case, how do we change ourselves in a radical way to be ready to educate this 2020 college student?'.

That tough question led us to ask what risks we were prepared to take. What values were we prepared to renegotiate? And what would be—and I use this over and over—the "gripping language" that would allow us to create an enlarged horizon?

So we made a commitment. Johnson C. Smith University would go through radical transformation. That was a turning point for all of us. I'm a firm believer that we often make mistakes by talking about strategic plans before we have a scenario. So I said, 'Why don't we describe—*envision*—all these processes we're talking about?'. That's where the concept of the "independent new urban university" emerged, a concept that had been written about by Jake Shrum. The title was *Democracy's Last Stand*. He said that if we do not create universities around certain core principles, we will fail at our overriding purpose to protect democracy.

When we looked at our history from the Biddle Institute at Johnson C. Smith University, all our core values related to the defining characteristics of an "independent new urban university". So that became our scenario. From there, we started looking at every aspect of the university in terms of how we would co-create this new reality, how we would finance it, what risks we would have to take. We knew that we would be on a bumpy ride; nevertheless, we had the courage and vision to do it. Because we can become this dream, we can become this vision, and in becoming this vision, we can add to the knowledge base of the country.

[3] Martin Van Der Werf and Grant Sabatier, 'The College of 2020: Students', 19 June 2009, http://blogs.lt.vt.edu/inventthefuture2020/the-college-of-2020-students/

How would you describe the leadership structure you created?

We have to work hard to first make sure that everyone understands the vision. We have to work with them to embrace the vision once they understand it. And then we've got to get them to become it. All three must be in place if this radical transformation is going to take place.

In order to understand it, we have to engage in "representative thinking". It is not my vision; it is the university's vision. It represents our best thinking. In order for you to give substance to best thinking, you cannot have a subsidiary model of management, where the president speaks to the trustees and then turns and speaks to his administrative team, and the administrative team then speaks to their managers, and the managers then speak to the staff, and the staff speaks to the students. That is not the way it works. If you want to engage in representative thinking you must have cross-functional teams that have authority. So we made a commitment that we would have a flat organizational structure here at Smith that would be managed by groups that are cross-functional. Then we say to everyone, 'It's my responsibility". We have to be accessible, we have to be out there so people can embrace what we are talking about.

I said to the deans, 'You are going to become a council of deans. You are going to work together to solve problems in common', and that way we don't have layers in the academy. Conflict is good as long as you engage in the conflict for a better purpose. Conflict has a high value in radical transformation, but it is not conflict without trusting each other, being patient with each other, being willing to raise tough questions, being committed to our good failures. That's what we facilitate in radical change, and that's the role of positive failure, because it tells us there's still something missing. Take it, go back, and innovate around it.

How did you frame your vision for this work? What was the story you told about why this was important?

Why do we do what we do? For what good purpose? When we wrestle with those questions, we see that we have to be intellectually honest. I can talk about quality education, but I ask, 'For what purpose?'. Is it to screen out those I perceive to not be contributing to quality? And with this sanitized version, and with students already ordained to succeed, can I then say this is "quality" because I have screened out those who do not contribute? Or do I need to rethink the very meaning of quality, so that it's inclusive and it's diverse? When I look within and then look out, my commitment is to diversity and inclusion. The purpose of education is to give everybody a common ground where they can grow their capacity, and as teachers and administrators, we are nutrients to fertilize the soil in which that person is growing. We are there to attend to their growth possibilities.

We realized if we were really going to be diverse and inclusive, we could not continue with traditional standards in admitting students. We started looking at this concept of "non-cognitive variables". We acknowledged there were cognitive variables. Then we said, 'There are meta-cognitive variables; that's the intersection where the cognitive and non-cognitive meet'. That becomes a strength perspective. We were saying, 'Why not admit students on *their* strength perspective of themselves? What are we capable of doing to help them realize it?'. All of a sudden, we were seeing a new way of educating students who had been excluded, and by golly they were doing just as well as the students who came the traditional way. We're living the longitudinal study. Now we're saying, 'We can become a new urban university committed to diversity and inclusion. We have access points for all students, and we can educate them to excellence'.

We have to wrestle with how to bring in students who are not meeting traditional requirements without dumbing down anything. We said University College will be the place where liberal education will be taught, where students who have not declared a major will have a safe space to find their way to a major, and where students who've met some but not all of the criteria can be supported through intrusive advising.

Johnson C. Smith is an institution that lives, breathes, and promotes cultural competency for the good of the community. So we created a Master of Social Work programme that has a strong focus in an innovative way around cultural competency. Then we realized that could translate into everything we were doing at the university, which then says to the public at large, 'If you are looking to educate this new demographic, Johnson C. Smith is the best place to learn how to do it. We've been doing it for 150 years, and we have informed visions, and we're doing research'. And by golly we are going to get in the forefront because we're culturally competent to do it without embarrassment, without apology. That's how we see ourselves.

Education is not meant to screen; it is meant to include. And for what purpose? To use John Silber's words, to 'maintain the promise of democracy'. It's our responsibility to come up with new approaches that will break through traditional paradigms. We are constitutionally fit to be diverse and inclusive. And all who are like-minded, come. But if you want to be diverse and not inclusive, don't come here. Whether you are a faculty member, a wanna-be administrator, or even a student, just don't come.

We're standing around the fire, talking, and something emerges that we all realize: this is ours. I never told the story by myself because I have trustees who are with me telling the story. I have faculty, I have students, and we tell the story. When we tell the story that way, it becomes contagious. Other people want to just sit and listen and say, 'Well, I see something I can add to the story'. Come on in, sit down, stir the fire, and let's see what keeps coming out of it.

Johnson C. Smith University Visual Case Study

Sense-Making
To design this future institution, the leadership team examined other models for inspiration, such as the University College. Through robust community engagement, they ultimately created a solution unique to Johnson C. Smith, a design championed by President Carter.

Spark
In response to research showing that by 2020 most prospective college students would be minorities, the board of trustees challenged President Carter to transform the organization to ensure it would be prepared to educate this new demographic.

New Vision
As a natural expression of their mission as an HBCU, leaders reconsidered how their institution could dismantle systemic barriers and inequities in access to higher education. They designed innovative new criteria to evaluate applicants using "non-cognitive variables" to signal potential for success in higher education. These students would then receive wrap-around support to ensure their success.

Executive Leadership
President Carter guided the transformation through persistent and challenging questions and by pushing leaders to identify problems within each initiative. He developed "flat" cross-functional teams and a Deans Council. Carter understood that innovation at the university is not a linear process, but rather an iterative response to its environment.

Team/Mandate
To support and accelerate this transformation, groups were reorganized into cross-functional teams with broad decision-making authority, creating a "flat" organization. Values of courage and transparency were demonstrated throughout levels of leadership.

Iteration
Flat organizational structure allowed cross-functional teams to evaluate alternatives and make changes in design.

Johnson C. Smith University
The University College

THE BIDDLE INSTITUTE

Investigates and provides academic support to new students using the following strengths-based assessments:

- Biddle Freshman Program: "Support programming" that includes faculty-teaming, intrusive advising, academic success workshops, and 13 credit-hour limits
- Center for the Study of Metacognitive Variables: Research think-tank that studies non-cognitive and metacognitive skills as predictive factors for student success
- Sit Lux Initiative: Programme that mandates Biddle Freshman Program activities with intrusive mentoring and interventions

FIRST-YEAR EXPERIENCE

Supports students' transition to the university and the enrichment of academic skills.

LIBERAL STUDIES

Delivers the core curriculum.

Who They Serve

As a small private liberal arts university with HBCU traditions, Johnson C. Smith enrolls 1,600 students from diverse backgrounds.

Providing Access

Students admitted through the Biddle Institute must meet either the minimum GPA or standardized test score, as well as answer questions designed to assess non-cognitive assets.

Enabling Success

The University College provides a comprehensive experience designed to connect first-year students to the institution, preparing students for university life and beyond. In doing so, the College develops students' communication, reasoning, leadership, and career skills through three interrelated divisions: the First-Year Experience, the Biddle Institute, and Liberal Studies.

NATIONAL LOUIS UNIVERSITY
Chicago, Illinois

NLU launched the innovative *Harrison Professional Pathways Program* in Fall 2015 to address the disproportionate number of students from historically marginalized backgrounds who do not enroll in or complete college. It also serves as a scalable model for higher education, both locally and nationally. In its first year, the *Pathways Program* enrolled 85 freshmen and had 75% students return for sophomore year, exceeding local and national benchmark retention rates by offering an accessible price, holistic wraparound support services, and broad admissions criteria.

The NLU *Pathways Program* supports students who have been traditionally underserved in higher education. *Pathways* students are predominantly below college readiness levels, and the majority are first-generation, low-income, and Hispanic and African-American. Year 1 recruitment efforts targeted Chicago Public Schools' graduating seniors to enroll at NLU's Chicago campus, while Year 2 recruitment expanded to a broader range of both Chicago-area and suburban high schools surrounding NLU's Wheeling campus, where the programme was added that same year. *The Pathways Program* is well on its way to achieving its goal of serving nearly 5,000 undergraduate students by 2020, and to establishing a new undergraduate college. This approach to undergraduate education is designed to demonstrate that all students are capable of success if colleges become more "student-ready".

'We weren't going to last if we kept doing what we were doing. That led us to–in a pioneering way– break a lot of ground'.

'Other institutions in our tier are focused on rankings. We made a choice that we will focus on how well we serve our students.'

– President Nivine Megahed

NIVINE MEGAHED
President of National Louis University

Nivine Megahead, born in Egypt, grew up in New York State. She earned her BA in Psychology from the State University of New York at Buffalo, and an MA and PhD in Clinical Psychology from the University of Rochester. She began her academic career at the Georgia School of Professional Psychology and was a campus dean at the American School of Professional Psychology in Hawaii. She also worked as a psychologist in private practice and as an educational and programmatic consultant for universities around the world. She has been president of multiple institutions, including the University of Sarasota and Kendall College in Chicago. In 2010, Megahed became the eleventh president of National Louis University.

Her current strategic priorities include providing affordable, accessible, quality education that promotes student success; focusing on veterans' education; expanding new frontiers in digital education; and growing the university's leadership in community-based applied research that focuses on schools as a central base for community transformation.

Interview with

NIVINE MEGAHED

This Interview Has Been Edited and Condensed for Clarity

How has your personal journey informed your motivations to do this work?

I am trained as a clinical psychologist, but in every role I always thought about how to do it better and make the system work better. The big theme that drove me was that I always wanted to make a difference, to leave some kind of impact that is positive.

When I went to Hawaii, it was a campus that was in deep, deep trouble. It had never been fully accredited, and students were upset because they felt they had been promised things that weren't delivered. The faculty was disenfranchised. It was a big old mess. I didn't know any better, I just went in and said, 'Well, let's fix it. Let's get accredited and let's get people working together'.

That was it. That was my trajectory. Once I did that, I realized how much I loved impacting a system in that way and seeing all the lives you could improve if you really thought about what you needed to do at a higher level to make those changes. I loved the idea of building a great team that worked together, moving together towards something they all wanted. Eventually, I was tired of being in the for-profit space, because in the end there was always a stakeholder I didn't want to deal with, which was either a stockholder who wanted return on their investment or an owner who wanted more but didn't want to reinvest into the school, the students, or the programmes. I finally decided I wanted to work somewhere that's mission-driven. When the National Louis opportunity emerged, I was delighted.

What does *innovation* mean to you in the context of your work as an institutional leader?

Many feel that innovation is synonymous with technology, but I don't. I think of innovation as putting things together in a new way that helps either change the way you do things or the way the work is done. It's bringing together new concepts that help advance your goal. It's about challenging the norms and the status quo to create something. Our institution is a very innovative place, but only because we take nothing for granted.

I read a book in college, the classic, Thomas Kuhn's *The Structure of Scientific Revolutions*, which is about innovation because it's about suddenly realizing, 'Oh, the world doesn't sit like this; it sits like this'. Then all of a sudden everything changes because you recognize the world is round, it's not flat. We're on the periphery, we're not in the center. That's innovation. It's looking at it so differently that it forces you to do everything else differently.

How did you experience the severity of external pressures on your institution?

We were facing the same kind of economic headwinds that most of our sector had been facing for the last several years. That led us to do all kinds of courageous things. When I came on, we were one of the first to do a programme review and evaluation, and we shut down programmes because enrollment and revenue had dropped, and we were still tuition-dependent. We reviewed all our programmes, we involved the entire community, and we shut down 15 programmes. We dramatically reduced the number of faculty and staff. We probably cut our size by a third. I remember my president peers (in Chicago, there are so many presidents—there are so many universities) kept saying, 'We're watching, you're not going to last'. And I kept saying, 'Well, we weren't going to last if we kept doing what we were doing'.

I believe necessity is the mother of invention, but that led us to—in a pioneering way—break a lot of ground. We started rebuilding and driving towards a much more disciplined, deliberate, metrically-driven culture—a culture that made decisions based on evidence as opposed to instinct. There was a lot of trial and error trying to figure out the best way to position ourselves. I recognized that our strongest route was sticking to our core commitments, our "mission commitments". If we stayed true to those, it was the right thing. Our mission commitments were about serving students, helping them impact their communities. It was about access for students. I mean, this institution was built on a mission of access for everybody.

How do you do that in the highest quality way? You pull it apart and see what nuggets of truth you should address. If we're really going to achieve our mission commitments, then we should be concerned about the cost, we should be concerned about whether the students finish, and we should be concerned if our teachers are prepared when they enter the classroom.

And that's when clarity hit, like, 'Stop! You don't need to fight this; you need to solve it'. So we started. One morning four or five years ago I said, 'I want to create an affordable education for people'. I saw the sociodemographics changing, and I said, 'People have to access it'. I mean, 87% of our kids in Chicago Public Schools—400,000 of them—are low-income. Across the state, 50% of our kids are low-income. How do you provide access if people can't afford to go there? I started on this idea and pulled together a couple people and hired someone from the outside. I said, 'I want to create an affordable degree, but I also want it to be better quality than what we have. I want it to be able to scale, I want it to improve completion rates against the national average, and I want employment rates that are outstanding'.

We tapped into an unmet need because it's a completely diverse population we serve. We tapped into it with everything we learned at the institution, so we tapped into it with incredible analytics all the way through. What's predicting student success? How do we get at grit? How do we improve the mindset? How do we see their engagement in the classroom? We have measures for everything, and we're tracking it all, and we're learning so much as we go. As the sample gets larger, we see which things are robust and which are not. It's set up in a context where there's rapid iterations, so in Year 1 we saw we needed to give them a week to ramp up. When Year 2 students came in the second freshman year, we told them we're starting a week earlier. We called it Ramp Week.

Every month I take a group of students to lunch, and I sit and talk with them. I'll say, 'Tell me about who you are or what you want to do, what's important to you'. I find it baffling that every university isn't jumping in trying to serve this population, because 90% of them leave you awed. Every one of them I talked to—what just blows my mind—wants to go back, to make their communities better.

How many students coming from these blighted neighborhoods, who have no opportunity, how many of them do we have to educate, graduate, and help get employed for them to want to be back in their communities, to change their social and economic opportunities? How many of them need to go back into their communities to change the communities? That's what we're going to do here: We are going to show how to really impact communities. It's through education, but it's by supporting people all the way to their employment. It's not, 'Okay, you graduated, you're done'. We have to be accountable to their connection to employment.

You can't be good at everything. On occasion one must choose to be bad at some things. Does this idea have merit for you as a leader? How has it played out in your organization?

I constantly say to people that we can only work on two or three things at a time, and those should be what we drive the hardest. Don't worry about everything else. It's not about choosing to be bad; it's about focusing on what you want to build. It's hard to keep people focused on the thing they want to be great. We decided we wanted to be great at this undergrad initiative, and I've ensured focus by creating a dedicated team of resources.

How would you describe the leadership structure you created?

In the first few years, every decision was coming to me while we were in crisis. Everything kept bubbling up, little or big, and people were afraid to make decisions. At a certain point, when we got out of the worst of it, I said, 'All right, we're not about to be extinct, so I want you all to lead. It's not just me making all these decisions'. We made leadership team adjustments, and we finally got the right team in place. There were a couple messages that went out. One was that I wanted the leaders to lead their units and empower their people to lead, but I also wanted a lot of collaboration across units. So, I got the right people to put that together.

I expected everyone to be a decision-maker. They should never punt on a decision. The most stagnating thing for an organization is when people won't decide. In higher education people like to fall back and do not want to decide. You have to counteract that. I said in all decisions, 'You make the best decision you can, but I want your decision-making to be guided by this: Are you making the decision that is in the best interest of our students?'. We changed the culture. There's nothing we cannot fix if it's the wrong decision, but we cannot fix indecision. Success is built on a pile of failure.

I had to build the team, and it took a little while to get right. There were a few fits and starts where it wasn't a right match and we had to make a change. I have a developmental approach to an executive team. I see them as effective in certain phases, then they probably need to either move on to greater things or move on to something different, because as you hit a different ramp, you're no longer playing to their strengths.

How did you frame your vision for this work? What was the story you told about why this was important?

My first few years here, the feedback was that folks didn't feel they had a vision. We were in crisis, so it's harder to come up with a vision when you're making sure you don't capsize. It's one of those things that I grew into, as opposed to *Ta da here's the vision!*

At the end of the day, when I think about what drives us, it's because we believe every child deserves a great teacher, and we believe that every individual deserves an opportunity for economic prosperity and social mobility. But how do we manifest those beliefs?

We try to own the entire lifecycle of education because we believe that's the greatest lever for economic and social opportunity, and it starts with making sure every kid has a great teacher in K-12. We started out as a teacher prep organization; we were the first school for teachers in this state. We have to stay on top of developing great teachers for the kids of Illinois and this nation, and we have to always provide access and opportunity for individuals to impact their communities.

I realized that most of the time we talked about *impact* as, 'Well, our students do well and graduate'. That's a good outcome, but that's not the impact. As an institution we've always been pioneering and dedicated to innovation, but we've also always been in the service of supporting students and impacting our communities. I started recognizing that it's bigger than just graduating our students. It's about how we change these communities. How is education a lever that does that? How is education the thing that helps people achieve the sort of economic prosperity that drives broader change for everybody?

National Louis University Visual Case Study

Sense-Making

The university was then faced with the challenge to rebuild and redesign. President Megahed grounded this effort in a deep commitment to the university's mission. She initiated a monthly listening session with students to learn more about their lives and what was important to them.

Spark

National Louis University was facing economic pressure and a declining enrollment. In response to this pressure they conducted a robust programme review involving the entire community. This resulted in the difficult decision to cut fifteen programmes, reducing the size of the institution by almost a third.

New Vision

Anchored in its existing mission to provide broad access, serve its students, and help them impact their communities, NLU achieved its new vision by centering the student experience and making evidence-based decisions.

Executive Leadership

President Megahed provided directive and strategic leadership during restructuring, then pivoted to a more distributed model during rebuilding. Leaders were empowered to make unit-level decisions and collaborate across silos. The result was a culture that supported bold decisions and prioritized students' best interests.

Team/Mandate

Teams were encouraged to be bold in their decisions, and to ground their decisions in evidence and data. Work was prioritized to a few key projects at a time to create focus. Underlying all of their efforts was the belief that "if you put in the effort, you will succeed." University leaders and faculty held this belief for themselves and their work to reinvent the university, just as they held it for their students and their potential to succeed.

Iteration

As university employees witnessed the review process and redesign efforts, more took risks to innovate and improve, leading to a culture of continuous improvement and success.

National Louis University Professional Pathways Program

PERSONALIZED INSTRUCTION

Adaptive online curriculum replaces textbooks, engaging students at their various levels. Face-to-face classes feature small class sizes so that professors truly get to know students and provide individualized support.

FLEXIBILITY

Pathways courses meet twice weekly so students can complete most of the work on their own schedules.

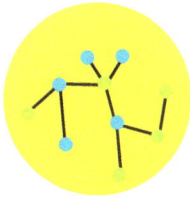

DATA

Professors and coaches meet weekly to review student data and plan interventions. Administrators review data twice per quarter to inform ongoing enhancements to the programme.

PATHWAYS

Pathways takes the guesswork out of course selection, providing clear and efficient tracks toward graduation.

COACHING & MENTORING

Success Coaches provide personal, academic, and career support and guidance, helping students stay on track to graduate.

Who They Serve

The NLU *Pathways Program* serves students who have traditionally been under-served in higher education; predominantly first-generation college-goers, low-income, and Hispanic and African-American students.

Providing Access

At $10K a year, Pathways is the most affordable bachelor's degree programme in Illinois. A minimum GPA of 2.0 is the only admissions criteria.

Enabling Success

Real-time student data enable high-touch student support and intervention and highly personalized instruction and pathways to graduation.

https://doi.org/10.11647/OBP.0157.05

GEORGIA STATE UNIVERSITY
Atlanta, Georgia

Over the course of five years, Georgia State University created a new type of data-informed advising platform, Graduation Progression Success (GPS) Advising, which identifies more than 800 challenges and tracks every student daily for emerging problems. University initiated a Summer Success Academy for students underperforming in high school, and introduced Panther Retention Grants (PRG) to cover the gap between what college students can pay and the full cost of their tuition and fees, helping students stay enrolled.

Because of a data-informed, campus-wide commitment to student success, Georgia State's graduation rate improved 22 percentage points over ten years. Rates are up 36 points for Latinos (to 58%) and 29 points for African-Americans (to 58%). Latino, African-American, low-income, and first-generation students now all graduate at rates at or above the overall student body—not just narrowing achievement gaps, but closing them. Georgia State now confers bachelor's degrees to more Hispanic, Asian, first-generation, and low-income students than any other university in Georgia. For the last six years, it has conferred more bachelor's degrees to African-Americans than any other non-profit college or university in the United States.

'We have to educate the students we get. It can't be like when I showed up to college and they said, "Look to your left, look to your right. In four years one of you won't be here". That's no longer acceptable. […] Our mission is to provide a level playing field for all students, so that education contributes to closing the gap between haves and have-nots that's dividing our nation today'.

– *President Mark P. Becker*

MARK P. BECKER
President of Georgia State University

As a first-generation college student who began at a community college, Mark P. Becker is personally and professionally committed to helping students from all economic backgrounds to succeed. He attended Harford Community College in Maryland and earned his BS in Mathematics from Towson State University, and Doctorate in Statistics from Pennsylvania State University. He taught at the University of Washington and the University of Florida and spent over a decade at the University of Michigan's School of Public Health, also serving as associate dean for Academic Affairs. Becker was executive vice president for Academic Affairs and provost at the University of South Carolina, and dean of the School of Public Health at the University of Minnesota. He began his tenure as Georgia State University's seventh president in January 2009.

His ambitious vision has fueled Georgia State's emergence as one of the nation's premier urban research universities, which has helped revitalize downtown Atlanta and raise the university's global profile with international partnerships. Georgia State has become a national leader in innovating programmes and initiatives to foster student success; in eliminating disparities in graduation rates based on race, ethnicity or income; and in offering financial support to students. Georgia State was ranked the fourth most innovative university in the country by *U.S. News & World Report* in 2017.[2]

---

[2] 'Georgia State Fourth Most Innovative University in U.S. News and World Report Best Colleges Edition', Georgia State University News Hub, 12 September 2017, https://news.gsu.edu/2017/09/12/georgia-state-fourth-innovative-university-u-s-news-world-report/

Interview with

MARK P. BECKER

This Interview Has Been Edited and Condensed for Clarity

How has your personal journey informed your motivations to do this work?

It's an evolutionary process, as you would imagine. I decided I wanted to be a professor when I was an undergraduate. I did not go to a strong high school. The thing that set me apart was I was really good at math. It was the way my brain was wired. My parents wanted me to be an engineer, so I started at a community college engineering programme that fed into the University of Delaware and University of Maryland. Most of my classmates went on to be engineers.

I really enjoyed figuring out problems, hard problems, and I had the mathematical ability to do it, so I switched from engineering to physics to math, graduated in four years, and figured I was going to become a math professor. I got to graduate school and majored in statistics because of an interest in solving problems across a range of disciplines. I had a specific interest in health care.

In my first faculty position as Assistant Professor of Statistics, I did a very unusual thing and took a leave from my tenure-track position that got me in the field of biostatistics and public health. There was again this sense of wanting to address substantive problems, not just academic ones.

My transition from faculty to higher education leadership happened at the University of Michigan. President Duderstadt knew higher education was going to change a lot. I was on a committee that regularly met with him. I learned the man was prescient and understood the challenges facing higher education, and I wanted a seat at the table when higher education faced those changes.

I had this sense back in the mid-1990s that we couldn't let a changing world destroy what is probably the most important asset this country has, a very rich higher education system that doesn't work as a system per se. It's not tightly integrated, but there is an opportunity for everybody. Whether it's Harvard, Yale, or a community college, everybody can get into the system. It's a mistake to think everything should be the same. The real strength of American higher education is its heterogeneity. We need a range of institutions that meets people where they are when they are ready to pursue an education.

My father was a soldier, my mother was a secretary, and my brothers and I were the first in our family to go to college. Higher education had created opportunities for us. Out of three boys we've got two with PhDs and one with a master's degree who was a colonel in the US Army and had a highly successful career in the Department of Defense. That's okay for three kids who benefited from public higher education.

When this opportunity at Georgia State presented itself, something inside me said the important change in the 21st century is going to happen in cities. Urban universities have to be a part of that.

How did you experience the severity of external pressures on your institution?

For better or worse, this wasn't the first time I was in a leadership role in a recession. The metaphor was, 'Look, we're in a storm, we're being tossed about. It's dark, the clouds are swirling, and we're on a sailing ship. Our responsibility is to get things in order so that when the storm clears we're headed in the right direction with wind in our sails'. It was a very difficult time, but it was also an opportunity to position the university for what we would do after the recession.

I was offered the job in October 2008, not a good time for the country economically, but it was also leading up to the historical election of an African-American president. I chose as my start date 1 January 2009. While I was preparing to become a president, there was a lot of buzz about the first 100 days of the Obama presidency, and it got me thinking. If the president of the United States has a first 100 days, so does a president of a university. I did what any modern person would do. I went to Amazon and typed in 'first 100 days' and found a plethora of books on those first 100 days. The recurrent theme was the need to know the heart and soul of the organization you're going to be responsible for. The books in different ways recommended going through a structured interview process, a listening process, in your first fifty to sixty days as you work toward coming up with a language, a vocabulary, for what you hope to achieve–your vision.

I settled on a basic five-question interview: 'What do you most value about Georgia State University?', 'What do you most want to see change?', 'What are you most hoping I will do?', and 'What are you most afraid I will do?'. And that fifth question, 'Is there anything else you want to talk about?'. I conducted that interview over the first thirty to forty days with thirty different campus leaders, the president of student government, the chair of our staff counsel, the executive committee of our university senate, the deans, and the vice presidents. What really stood out to me and became clear when I analyzed the results was that in 29 of the 30 interviews, what respondents most valued about Georgia State was the diversity of the student body, and that includes race and ethnicity. But there's more to it than that.

They started talking about non-traditional students, military learners, because Georgia has a large military presence, people of all ages, of all social and economic statuses, races, and ethnicities. It hit me that there was something about Georgia State that was not like any other university where I had worked. I'd spent my faculty career in flagship institutions. This was clearly very different, so the goal was to capture that and turn it into a strength and a distinctive feature of the institution.

Factoring in our urban environment and the diversity of our students, we crafted a vision that we were going to create an urban university that would have the features of a premier research university, but with a very different student body and a deeply committed faculty and staff. We undertook a lengthy strategic planning process in February 2010. We used a broadly inclusive process because we committed to using the resulting strategic plan to drive the budget, which we've done every year since then. We kicked that process off with a public presentation where I drew on Apple's famous 'Think Different' campaign.

My message was, 'Okay, we're going to do the strategic plan, we're going to use it to advance this university, and we're going to have to think differently'. You know, crazy things can be achieved–crazy in the sense that they're out of the ordinary, not crazy in that they're impossible.

The first semester of 2010 the planning process was very open. The committee conducted online surveys, wrote white papers, held town hall forums, had lots of discussion, and collected ideas. The only constraint I put on the process was that we could have no more than five goals because people can't remember more than that, and you have to fit it on one sheet of paper. If it's so complicated we can't get it down to a sheet of paper, we're not going to be able to use it.

We tested out drafts with external stakeholders, including major donors, elected officials, leaders of not-for-profits who would be partners, and potential supporters. The interviewees were unanimous in their assessment. The plan sounded impressive to them, but they didn't know what it meant and didn't know why they should care about it. The strategic planning committee was distraught. They said, 'Does this mean we start over?'. I said, 'No, that's not what they told you. What they told you is that they don't know what it means, and they don't know why they should care, because you wrote it in our academic language. I'll try to rewrite these five goals in a language that will be more broadly understood, and people will get a sense of what we're talking about and why they should care'.

At that point, increasing graduation and retention rates was Goal 3. We were already getting some progress with student success work, so my instinct was if we made this a real priority, it would be something worth doing. There would be tremendous value from a social justice point of view and as an economic imperative, and success would enable the university to distinguish itself in a way that is natural for an urban institution with a diverse student population.

When the plan was approved by our university senate in January 2011, our goal was a 60% graduation rate. I think at that time we were in the low 40s. It was going be a heavy lift, but once we got there, we'd set our sights on 100%. I know that's probably not realistic, but if we don't aim for it, we're going to become complacent and fall short.

How would you describe the leadership structure you created?

I'm naturally an impatient person. This "things playing out over a long period of time" horizon was something I had to learn. It goes back to when I was an associate dean; I became an associate dean expecting to become a dean. I figured it would take me three years. Well, I was an associate dean for five years and then became a dean. I realized I had learned much more in years four and five than I'd learned in the first three. And I realized if you want lasting change, if you really want to change something for the long term so it sticks, you've got to invest a lot of time. It takes time.

As president I have a cabinet, people who report directly to me and have major areas of responsibility. I've restructured the cabinet in various ways. We now have a chief innovation officer. It is a technology role, but it's focused on how we use technology to change what we do and how we do it. The big addition to the cabinet was the vice president for enrollment management and student success who manages everything from student recruitment to graduation. We put career services in that portfolio because, in my mind, career services are linked to the academic programme. They are linked to our student advising model now because students start with career advising as freshmen. We also have an administrative council. It's the deans, the VPs, and the associate provosts. We do a report on enrollment every week and ask ourselves what obstacles we're facing. We're not resting on our laurels. We're going after whatever is the next thing.

I've flattened the administrative structure. I have more direct reports, but I don't micromanage people. The hardest thing for me, for making the change from being an academic to being a leader, was letting go. Your success early in your career as a professor was determined by what you did. You got credit for your individual accomplishments.

Over time I've learned that if I empower people by hiring people with talent and giving them room to spread their wings, we'll all enjoy the benefits. And that's certainly worked. I ask lots of questions, but I don't call people up every day or require frequent reports. If somebody's not performing, I find somebody else to do the job. You've got to surround yourself with good people.

Skilled hiring is part of building a strong management team, but so is the commitment to fire ineffective people because you cannot do the disservice to the organization to keep people in roles where they don't belong. If you can't do that, you're never going to get where you want to go. It's recognizing you can't be all things to all people, as an individual and as an institution. I accept that I can't make everybody happy, but I'm always going to be very clear about our goals and priorities.

One lesson I've learned in higher education is if you get the process right, you can do just about anything. The faculty will embrace a lot of new ideas if you get the process right. If you don't get it right, you can end up with a brilliant idea that leads to great controversy.

How did you frame your vision for this work? What was the story you told about why this was important?

One priority was to organize our language so everyone would clearly understand our priorities. My first year became the first year in its history the university had more tuition revenue than state funding. The recession had taken $40 million out of our budget. It was clear to me the state was not going to be our savior. We had to get our message out. We had to get it out right, and we had to raise a lot more money than we were raising.

Our vision was to become a premier urban research university. We spent a lot of time telling people Georgia State was becoming a "complete university". *Transformation* was the word I used a lot. We were going to transform Georgia State into a real major research university that would be accessible to all college-ready students.

One of the unique features of Georgia State is the recent consolidation of Georgia Perimeter College, a two-year institution, into the university. Just about everybody who applies to Georgia State gets an admissions letter. The letter says you're admitted into a bachelor's degree programme at the Atlanta Campus or you're admitted into an associate degree programme at one of our Perimeter College campuses of your choosing. We admit everybody, but there are different pathways based on their preparation.

We have to educate the students we get. It can't be like when I showed up at college and they said, 'Look to your left, look to your right. In four years one of you won't be here'. That's no longer acceptable. Back then, college was almost free. Now these students are taking on substantial debt. Our mission is to provide a level playing field for all students, so that education contributes to closing the gap between haves and have-nots that's dividing our nation today.

I've told everybody here that the whole country's watching us. We've got to get it right. Not because the country is watching, but because it is crucial for the thousands of people across the nation who are flunking or dropping out of college.

There's no unique way to do things, but we've established a model that has been recognized nationally for demonstrating that students from all backgrounds can achieve and graduate at high rates. That has given us a powerful story to tell when we go to the Board of Regents for funding increases. Our priorities align with our university system strategic plan. Not surprisingly, the Board of Regents also has a graduation goal. We need more college-educated people, especially in Georgia and specifically the Atlanta metro area. The new jobs being created are for people with bachelor's degrees and above.

Students who come to Georgia State tend to be very gritty, very practical, very much about getting the education to make a better life. We are a practical institution. We are very strong academically, but we're not an "ivory tower". We want to level the playing field and provide an outstanding education in a research-rich environment in a way that connects to and takes advantage of this city.

When we started all this at Georgia State, I think some people thought I was crazy. 'We're Georgia State', they'd say. 'We can't say we're going to do something at the national level. That's just not who we are. That's not how it works. We love these students, but we've got to be realistic about what's possible'. So, borrowing a phrase from Steve Jobs, I adopted a "reality distortion field". If you want to accomplish something people think is impossible, you must zone in on it and believe with all your heart you're going to do it. It doesn't always work, but it's worked in our innovative student success initiatives and our rapid development into a major research institution. We've done things people didn't think possible.

Georgia State University Visual Case Study

Sense-Making

President Becker designed a collaborative strategic planning process to ensure faculty support. He challenged the planning committee to "think different" and shared stories of ambitious transformation to set a high standard. To focus efforts, the planning committee was constrained to five aspirational goals. The committee collected ideas from across the university through surveys, town halls, and open discussions.

Spark

President Becker joined GSU amid a recession and political climate that demanded cutting costs and doing a better job of serving students of color as well as low-income and first-generation students. In his first 100 days he conducted more than 60 listening sessions, which led to a strategic planning process.

New Vision

The university emerged with a vision to increase its graduation rate to 60 percent without changing its student body profile. To accomplish this vision, Georgia State developed a platform to rigorously investigate student outcome data, and to use this data to design and implement innovative strategies and programs.

Executive Leadership

President Becker set ambitious goals and empowered staff and administration to solve problems with guidance on priorities and reduced bureaucratic barriers. One employee described the atmosphere as 'extremely empowering and helpful because the team knows that if they made a good argument and can show something to be helpful, it doesn't have to go through layers of bureaucracy to make it happen'.

Team/Mandate

The focal point of the innovation was a data-driven, centralized advising system. The advisors' role was reimagined with high performance expectations. The organizational structure was streamlined to be more focused on advising and student's needs. A culture of freedom and autonomy to deliver accompanied a commitment to let go of those not contributing to the organization's success.

Iteration

Data is used to continuously improve advising interventions and campaigns and test new strategies.

Georgia State University Improving Graduation Rates

SUMMER SUCCESS ACADEMY

A seven-week summer programme is offered for students who perform poorly in key high school classes. Students take college-level courses and receive tutoring, advising, and academic and financial skills training.

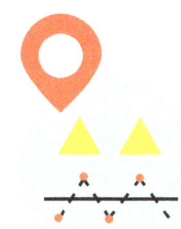

GPS ADVISING

The Graduation Progression Success (GPS) Advising platform tracks student data daily to flag risks and support aggressive advising.

DATA

In the face of changing demographics and declining funding, Georgia State asked some simple questions: What if we took student outcomes data seriously? What if we used data to diagnose why students were dropping out, then innovated and applied interventions to keep students on track to graduate?

PANTHER RETENTION GRANTS

Small awards cover the gap between the cost of tuition and fees and what students can pay.

Who They Serve

The Georgia State student body is broadly diverse in terms of age, social and economic background, race, ethnicity, and military status.

Providing Access

Every applicant to Georgia State receives an admittance letter. Students enter either a bachelor's degree programme at the Atlanta Campus or an associate degree programme at one of the university's Perimeter College campuses, which prepares them to transition to the Atlanta campus or transfer to another college or university.

Enabling Success

Georgia State uses robust real-time data modeling and aggressive advising to diagnose at-risk indicators. To drive student success, the university is committed to continuous innovation of its advising and intervention model.

https://doi.org/10.11647/OBP.0157.06

DELAWARE STATE UNIVERSITY
Dover, Delaware

Delaware State University (DSU) undertook a comprehensive effort to reimagine its university around ideals embedded in its strategic plan entitled *PRIDE 2020*. In doing so, the board of trustees and the president initiated efforts to increase retention rates to the national average (80%) and to change benchmark standards for graduation rates from six to four years.

To accomplish these goals, DSU developed a programme of individual development plans (IDPs) to personalize the progression of each student at DSU. An easy-to-use, flexible, computer-based tool generated a comprehensive composite of each student's profile data and performance. This tool provided advisors timely data to track individualized plans for student success, and DSU was able to create reports showing retention and graduation rates by college and programme.

The University College was created to support first-year students and simultaneously create a climate for success throughout their time at DSU. Each student has access to at least two IDP sessions with advisors/counselors, who focus on supporting students' individual goals, which is critical to first-year success.

Through these personalized, strategic efforts, DSU has already shown indicators of stronger student engagement, a proven factor in improving retention. DSU data has shown an increased fall-to-spring retention by 6 percentage points. Additionally, advisors and students report greater satisfaction due to new access to tools for tracking performance and regular check-ins for student engagement.

'Our students are first-generation, most of them low-income. Some, but not a lot, may have academic challenges in their background. […] They're waiting for someone to say they're not smart, they're waiting for someone to confirm these insecurities. But when you have someone that says, "You can do it", that's powerful'.

– President Harry L. Williams

HARRY L. WILLIAMS
President of Delaware State University
Years of Service: 2010–2017

Harry L. Williams has a BS in Communication Broadcasting and an MA in Educational Media, both from Appalachian State University, as well as an EdD in Educational Leadership and Policy Analysis from East Tennessee State University. He worked in admissions and did research at North Carolina Agricultural and Technical State University, which led to several leadership posts at Appalachian State University. Williams served as the tenth president of DSU from 2010–17, fulfilling a career-long goal of becoming president of a historically black college or university (HBCU). He currently serves as the President and Chief Executive Officer of Thurgood Marshall College Fund.

His visionary goals, focused on student success, have led to record-breaking growth in student numbers. His "friend-raising" efforts have also attracted numerous grants and increased state capital funding and a myriad of public/private partnerships, including exchanges and relationships with universities outside the United States. In early 2017, *HBCU Digest* named Williams among the 'Top 10 Influential HBCU Presidents'.[1]

---

[1] 'DSU President Harry Williams Honored by HBCU Digest', *Dover Post*, 4 January 2017, http://www.doverpost.com/news/20170104/dsu-president-harry-williams-honored-by-hbcu-digest

Chapter 6: **Delaware State University** | 49

Interview with

HARRY L. WILLIAMS

This Interview Has Been Edited and Condensed for Clarity

How has your personal journey informed your motivations to do this work?

It's been a strategic and deliberate journey because that was my goal, to be a college president. More specifically, it was my goal to be a college president at a historically black college and university (HCBU). That was my passion that drove me to this kind of work.

My background is education; I have an educational leadership degree. I worked for and attended and graduated from historically white institutions, so I never attended an HBCU, but it's always been something at the back of my mind in terms of the focus and the mission. They have always been organizations that focus on providing opportunities for those who may not have opportunities in other places. They were created out of that concept. These institutions were founded because blacks didn't have the legal right to go to schools with whites. The states had to do something to help ex-slaves get themselves out of their socioeconomic place. Education has always been that key to get you out.

I started working at my undergraduate university as an admissions counselor, where I needed a little knowledge about everything on campus, and that gave me a global perspective of the different disciplines and majors and different faculty members. I worked primarily recruiting minority students to attend this historically white institution. North Carolina was under a federal mandate, a federal consent decree: historically white institutions had to increase black enrollment by a certain percentage, and historically black institutions had to increase white enrollment by a certain percentage. If they didn't, the schools could risk losing federal funds. That intrigued me so much that I got my doctorate and did my dissertation on it. I wanted to look at whether that increased enrollment of blacks going college. I needed to work at a historically black college to collect my data. North Carolina Agricultural and Technical State University, which is in Greensboro, is the largest HBCU in America, and I got a job there as director of admissions. It gave me firsthand knowledge of the work and what was so important with it. I saw firsthand how that could change people's lives. It was the moment that I said, 'I want to be a college president'

As the director of admissions, I was sitting in the room at the Dean's Council and we had the dean of Engineering, the dean of the Graduate School, the dean of Arts and Sciences, the dean of Technology, the dean of the Nursing School, the provost, and me. Everybody around the table had PhDs from prominent institutions and they were all black. All black. Everybody. And I said, 'Wow'. I had always been in an environment where I was the only black person in a room of PhDs. Now I was in a room with black people with PhDs running a major institution. They could be at any other institution, but they were here. That gave me a sense of responsibility and I thought, these people made this decision because it's going to help, in particular, to be blunt, to pull a race up. At that moment I said, 'That's what I want to do'. I wrote a note to myself. I made goals. I said, 'I want to be president of an HBCU in ten years'. I was very specific. I knew what I needed to do in order to get that. So, in 2010, ten years later, I was the president at Delaware State.

What does *innovation* mean to you in the context of your work as an institutional leader?

When I think of innovation, I think of doing things that are not necessarily the same thing over and over. You're looking at different ways of how you approach things, having an open spirit and trying a variety of things without knowing if it's going to work. It's having the flexibility to make adjustments along the way, and using the creativity around you with people who have incredible experiences and incredible intellect in terms of how they might see and address a problem to improve a situation.

Technology is also driving a lot because it changes so fast and our students adapt. How do we make sure we're in line with those changes to support our students? I don't see the traditional college structure changing. It's a safe place where you can send your child at 18, where they can make a mistake, but that mistake is not going to be the detriment of their career. The role of the academic within the classroom, and more specifically within the discipline—you're going to need that. You're going to need that professor who's going to bring to the table all of his or her knowledge to help mold those students and develop those students at those critical developmental stages. That is an important part of a person growing into an adult.

How did you experience the severity of external pressures on your institution?

One of the challenges that we have at HBCUs, specifically working with first-generation college students, is how to support those individuals while recognizing that you can't put them in a certain box.

You have to take care of the day-to-day and you also have to think about sustainability. You have to think about the future and how long this is going to last. Part of that responsibility is that you have to do almost all those things simultaneously. You have to be able to balance what you can and can't do.

You also have to be able to say, 'I do this, right here, better than anybody, and since I do this better than anybody, this is going to be our key'. You can't jump at every new thing that comes along, because that takes you away from the focus area.

If you decide to be status quo, you're going to eventually die because status quo doesn't survive. But if you identify something that you want to be really, really good at, the other things around you will be pulled up. It's just like how winning is contagious. If you win, you like it, and then everybody wants to be a part.

How would you describe the leadership structure you created?

People value and respect and appreciate when you're honest with them, and when you're straightforward and not guessing. Part of my responsibility is to be honest and transparent and open so you know where I'm coming from.

My biggest thing is keeping people informed, speaking to the community, and keeping the community engaged with what we are doing. That's simple when you have three or four major initiatives you're pushing. One of the things that we have been focused on is student success. Everything that we do has got to be connected to that some way or another. My philosophy: If you commit, you commit. You have indicators of success along the way of that journey. When you get those indicators, that just reinforces that you're doing what's right.

When you are at a university with a lot of smart people, the worst thing to do is to put structure around them. You want smart people to have that freedom and flexibility to do things differently. As an administrator, my role is to make sure that if you come to me with an idea, I support that idea and will get the resources. I have to trust that you vetted it. I have to have the confidence in your ability to know what you need.

Some conflict is actually good for the organization, especially within the team. If you have a talented team, usually you have people pushing and pulling each other. As the leader, my job is to manage that process. I've got a lot of smart people sitting around my table. We've had people who haven't been able to get with the transformation. As part of that, we've lost some people along the way because of being stuck in their own ways of doing things.

We've been very successful in supporting our research scientists here, mainly because they are the ones who drive innovation. Part of that drive is having that talent to feel unconstrained by administrative matters. For a real academic, in my mind, that is minutia to them. My job is to make sure that we have procedures and policies in place that will allow for creativity to go uninhibited, where you won't have those challenges.

How did you frame your vision for this work? What was the story you told about why this was important?

When I became president, the first action I took was to create a vision for the institution. I was deliberate in creating that vision and making sure it was a shared vision within the community. I said I couldn't do anything else until this vision had been articulated so we all understood where we were going. You cannot develop a strategic plan if you don't have a vision.

The worst thing a leader can do is sit in their office and say, 'Okay, this is the vision I have for you'. It's got to be a community-engaged vision. This university was lacking clear focus, clear direction, so my job was to assemble a "blue ribbon task force" of major stakeholders of the university, people who believe in this institution. I had external people and internal. I had faculty, I had staff. Both of our senators are co-chairs, and we have one congressman, so we have three co-chairs of this blue ribbon commission. That gave it status. I did a listening tour around the state because we're a state university. We had focus questions in community town halls, asking, 'What do you want this university to look like?'.

We came up with five major core values that had already been at this institution but never written down. What do we believe as the core of our existence? Diversity, scholarship, integrity, community, and outreach. I tell all freshman when they come here, these are our values, this is what we believe in, and this is what we're going to do. This is what you're going to get from this institution.

The next step was to develop a strategic plan around that, which then becomes part of the community. I had 125 people involved in the strategic planning process. It took two years. We came up with clear goals, clear directions, so now we've got it. It's called *PRIDE 2020*. Now everybody builds their college-specific plan around the university plan.

Our students are first-generation, most of them are low-income. Some, but not a lot, may have academic challenges in their background because they may have made some mistakes along the way. But they've got some skills, they've got some talent. Having a professor understand that—because they're already coming in insecure, they're waiting for someone to say they're not smart, they're waiting for someone to confirm these insecurities. But when you have someone that says, 'You can do it', that's powerful.

Delaware State University Visual Case Study

Sense-Making

Through President Williams' leadership, this vision was co-created with the community. He assembled a 'blue-ribbon task force' of key internal and external stakeholders who conducted listening sessions around the state, engaging over 300 people in the process. Within 90 days they had created a vision for the university.

Spark

President Williams' first priority upon joining the university was to create a clear vision for the institution. He knew the university needed to be focused in its approach to student success and respond to the growing environmental pressures.

New Vision

The task force defined the university's new vision: to be the best historically black college in America and first choice of employers. They pursued this vision through five major core values: diversity, scholarship, integrity, community, and outreach.

Executive Leadership

President Williams clarified organizational priorities and created opportunities for staff and faculty to innovate. He eliminated barriers to success as identified by those working closest with students.

Team/Mandate

The new vision informed the collaborative strategic planning, which took two years and involved over 300 stakeholders. This process resulted in the launch of *PRIDE 2020* to improve student retention to 80% and shorten benchmark graduation rates from six to four years. Leadership focused on removing barriers so colleges and faculty could creatively focus on the university's shared priorities.

Iteration

To sustain organizational changes, faculty and staff held monthly forums to highlight student successes and key performance indicators (KPIs). These meetings reinforced a shared focus and provided opportunity for feedback and critical insights.

Delaware State University
University College

UNIVERSITY COLLEGE

The University College supports first-year students and creates a climate for success throughout their time at DSU.

COACHING & MENTORING

Real-time data supports direct and intrusive advising.

DATA

1. Individual Development Plans (IDP) include real-time data on student performance.

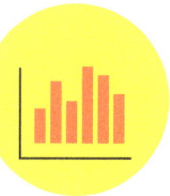

2. The Data Transformation team, including a dedicated data scientist continually improve on models to inform the IDP.

3. University-level key performance indicators (KPIs) enable performance-based management based on real-time data.

Who They Serve

Most of Delaware State University students are first-generation, low-income students.

Providing Access

This HBCU's admissions criteria for freshman students include a minimum 2.0 GPA and SAT score of 800.

Enabling Success

Individual Development Plans provide students, faculty, and advisors with real-time data, which enables intrusive advising and individualized student success planning. The University College provides intensive support for first-year students.

https://doi.org/10.11647/OBP.0157.07

MERCY COLLEGE
Main campus - Dobbs Ferry, New York

Mercy College's *Mercy Success Toolkit* focuses on six broad areas of activity, intended to improve student learning, persistence, graduation, and career placement. Mercy College's academic deans, faculty, and key administrative staff implemented the following strategies to increase student success:

Faculty Excellence: Opportunities for faculty to participate in professional development activities and engage with students outside the classroom

Course Redesign: Redesigned courses, which had typically served as "gatekeepers" to student success, by incorporating necessary math and English supports and remediation

PACT Mentoring and Targeted Interventions: Customized student support enabling the college to effectively monitor student progress and intervene as individually necessary to keep students on track

Choice Architecture: Utilization of Guided Pathways (GPS) for structure, built-in feedback, and support to help students make more informed choices without limiting their options

Multiply High Impact Educational Practices: Expanded active learning opportunities in the classroom, such as internships and project-based learning

Career Landing Paths: Foundation for students to launch their careers through internships, relationships with employers, and intersections between the career office and academic curriculum

'Is it better to go get better students, or to get better for the students we have? You have to make that choice. Most institutions make the choice of pursuing more academically talented students. This institution made the choice of getting better for the students we have'.

– President Tim Hall

TIM HALL
President of Mercy College

Timothy L. Hall received a BA in Philosophy from the University of Houston in 1978, followed by two years of graduate work in the Religious Studies department at Rice University in Houston, Texas, before attending law school and receiving his juris doctorate from the University of Texas Law School in 1983. After five years as a trial lawyer, Hall became a professor of law at the University of Mississippi, where he later served as associate vice chancellor of Academic Affairs. He then served for seven years as the president of Austin Peay State University in Clarksville, Tennessee, where he helped pioneer the innovative use of technology to support students. Hall became the twelfth president of Mercy College in 2014 and has focused on both increasing enrollment at the college's four campuses and promoting greater student success. His particular mission has been to reach out to traditionally underserved students in higher education, giving them the tools and technology for greater student retention. In 2015, Mercy College was recognized as one of the 'Bright Spots in Hispanic Education' by the *White House Initiative on Educational Excellence for Hispanics*.[4]

---

[4] 'The White House Designates Mercy College a Bright Spot in Hispanic Education', *Mercy College News*, 22 September 2015, https://www.mercy.edu/newsroom/white-house-designates-mercy-college-bright-spot-hispanic-education

Interview with

TIM HALL

This Interview Has Been Edited and Condensed for Clarity

How has your personal journey informed your motivations to do this work?

Out of law school I worked for a federal judge for one year, and then I practiced for five years as a trial lawyer, which is a pretty intense life. One year, one of my colleagues from the law firm applied and ended up becoming a law professor at Texas Tech University. The next year, three more of us applied from the same small office. One of us went to North Texas to become business faculty, one to Oklahoma, and I went to Mississippi.

After a number of years, I was invited to join the provost office at the University of Mississippi. I spent five years in that role and then made the move to Tennessee, where I was the president of Austin Peay State University. We'd been focused very much on student success and how to help more of our students persist to graduation. After about seven years at Austin Peay, I was trying to chart out the rest of my career. I had a dozen or so years left that I thought I would work, until I was 70. I was trying to understand whether I would stay there. People would have been very happy to see me stay. But I was worried that you couldn't do the job well for 20 years in one spot, so I started looking for another situation.

What does *innovation* mean to you in the context of your work as an institutional leader?

When I hear the phrase "change agent" it makes me want to put my hand on my wallet. I have frequently seen situations where somebody comes in with a vision of exactly what ought to happen. When everybody is startled and aghast at the speed of the changes and they complain about not being included, that person says, 'Well, that's what happens when you're an agent of change'.

How did you experience the severity of external pressures on your institution?

In my conversations with the search committee and then ultimately with the board at Mercy, it was clear that the board was very interested in student success. That was a priority for them. They deliberately considered whether they were looking for a president who would be primarily external and primarily engaged in fundraising, or a president who would be predominantly internal to help the institution front itself in ways that would be more conducive to the success of students.

They ultimately opted for the internal president who would be focused on helping the institution frame itself. I was very interested in that work. I had been engaged in it in Tennessee. It's some of the most important work going on right now. The traditional models of external presidents who aren't engaged in such work are out. For most institutions there's a lot of pressure and a lot of need to reframe themselves. That requires leadership inside. That's what Mercy wanted and that's what I wanted, so that's how we ended up together.

The broad context is that higher education over the last generation has increasingly discovered that institutions can be framed in ways that support the success of their student—or don't. Higher education was generally experiencing more financial stress, so the notion that an institution had the power to do things that would support students persisting, studying, and continuing to pay tuition all the way towards graduation was important. I don't think there was an institution that could ignore that. The narrow context was that Mercy's board knew who it was serving and had traditionally served the population of students that experienced special challenges, greater challenges, when it came to persistence and completion.

How would you describe the leadership structure you created?

I have this quotation from Lao Tzu that I learned in high school: 'A leader is best when people barely know he exists. When his work is done, his aim fulfilled, they will say: we did it ourselves'. That's been imprinted on my mind all my life.

I believe that all of us know more than any of us. That means that I lack knowledge, and the only way to get it is to build many bridges to people, so they can help me understand what I need to understand for my role. That means I don't view myself as the primary decision-maker. I view myself as the person who facilitates decisions getting made because you can't normally act unless you make some decisions.

In all sorts of everyday business, it's a matter of getting us to a decision. That means getting the right people talking, and understanding who's the right person to make a decision if it's not going to be some collective. This strategy comes from a legal background, where law is very much about understanding appropriate patterns of deference. Who deserves deference? Who is the right decision-maker for this particular point?

I'm not the best person to make all the decisions, I'm simply not. I saw that in law and now at the university. There will be people who come into my office constantly, wanting me to make decisions about the menu for a particular event, or the floral arrangements, or all sorts of other details. I constantly try to convey that I don't know anything about those matters. We need to get the people who know the most about those matters to make those decisions.

I think of the whole institution as predominantly like that. I'm not the best person to make a decision about whether some particular faculty member is scholarly productive in a discipline outside the one I know. That means I will always defer to other decision-makers unless I have some reason to think that something's broken, or unless somebody has to step in to cast a deciding vote.

Appropriate patterns of deference are crucial to helping the institution work. When you respect other decision-makers, that helps you lead more in your sphere, rather than when you appear to be somebody who's going to do it all yourself. Nobody respects that. They will put up with it if they have to, but nobody respects it. People respect the notion that I don't purport to know everything, that I will not try to make every decision, that I will respect other decision-makers. And that I will in fact encourage a place where we try to make, as much as possible, decisions collectively. I want a context where the greatest sin is not failing; it is not learning from failure. Failure is inevitable to progress.

Interview with Tim Hall

How did you frame your vision for this work? What was the story you told about why this was important?

I aspire to be a "servant leader", and that means I don't just fix the problems I see, but I'm able to be directed and focused by the people in this community towards the problems they see.

I come with the presupposition that one has to earn the right to speak persuasively. The most common way that occurs is by engaging with all the institution's constituents by listening very, very carefully to them so that they are not only inputting, but they are full partners in the work. While I was in Tennessee, that's the path I pursued, and I'm pursuing the same path here. It's more difficult here because we have multiple campuses. I probably spend a couple hundred hours a year in listening sessions with every academic department and every staff division, trying to hear what people perceive as our problems and our challenges and our opportunities.

I know that listening is an act of respect, but it loses a great deal of its value if people discover that there's no action that follows. The action piece is very, very important.

Every institution has a mission, and my experience most places is it doesn't mean anything because it's in a book someplace high on a shelf. Mercy's mission is spoken about constantly. It informs and guides things on a day-to-day level. People will say, 'I'm not sure that's consistent with our mission', or, 'This is what we have to do because of our mission'. Mission, especially understood to serve traditionally underserved students, is always at the forefront of Mercy. In fact, this is one of the things that drew me because most institutions that I've been a part of have this implicit notion that the solution to most of our problems is to get better students.

One of the things I was listening very closely to when I started interviewing with Mercy is whether that's the kind of president they were looking for, a president who will find better students and gradually migrate away from the demographics they currently served. I was very happy to discover that they clearly understood, no, that's not the goal. We understand getting better not as getting better students, but as getting better for the students we have. That's what getting better is about, and that's what they wanted: a president to help lead the community to get better for the students we have.

Mercy College Visual Case Study

Sense-Making
President Hall spent his first year identifying innovative grassroots efforts scattered across the organization that aligned with best practices in the field. He provided a framework to unite them as strategic priorities to enable focus, collaboration, and experimentation across the college.

Spark
The board mandated President Hall when he joined to focus internally to improve student persistence and completion, specifically for their student population, which faces greater challenges with academic success.

New Vision
'Defeat Demography' was Mercy's transformative rallying cry. This slogan refocused the college to improve its services and student outcomes, versus the traditional focus of "improving" the caliber of students accepted into the college.

Executive Leadership
Before stepping into his role, President Hall ensured he was aligned with the board of directors, that his leadership efforts would be focused internally to help the college redefine itself in service of student success. He delegated decisions to those who knew the most rather than relying on the traditional organizational hierarchy, and he encouraged a culture that could embrace failure in service of learning.

Team/Mandate
A clear and cohesive strategy enabled teams to act "in sync" across departments. President Hall enabled innovation across the college by prioritizing and funding distinct pilot programmes and by granting teams a high degree of autonomy. Collaboration was encouraged through team design and incentives.

Iteration
A culture of innovation continues to spread as learning-from-failure (rather than hiding it) becomes an organizational norm; pilot programmes scale naturally and rapidly through successful engagement of faculty, staff, and students.

Mercy College Mercy Success Toolkit

FACULTY EXCELLENCE

Faculty can participate in professional development activities and engage students outside the classroom.

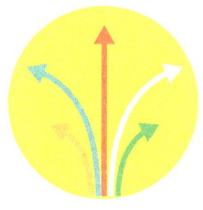

CHOICE ARCHITECTURE

Utilizing Guided Pathways (GPS), students receive structure, built-in feedback, and support to make more informed choices without limiting their options.

MULTIPLY HIGH IMPACT EDUCATIONAL PRACTICES

Active learning opportunities are expanded in the classroom, such as internships and project-based learning.

COURSE REDESIGN

Courses that typically had served as "gatekeepers" to student success were redesigned by incorporating math and English supports and remediation.

PACT MENTORING & TARGETED INTERVENTIONS

Customized student supports enable the college to effectively monitor student progress and intervene as individually necessary to keep students on track.

CAREER LANDING PATHS

Students are provided with the foundation to launch their careers through internships, relationships with employers, and intersections between the career office and academic curriculum.

Who They Serve

Mercy College students hail from diverse backgrounds and are largely first-generation college students.

Providing Access

Mercy College admits students based on a combination of academic achievement, leadership potential, extracurricular activities, and ability to contribute to the campus community. Standardized test scores are optional to their application.

Enabling Success

Mercy College's *Mercy Success Toolkit* is a set of strategies focused on six broad areas of activity, intended to improve student learning, persistence, graduation, and career placement. These strategies were designed to scale to all Mercy students rather than a subset considered high-risk.

https://doi.org/10.11647/OBP.0157.08

PORTLAND STATE UNIVERSITY
Portland, Oregon

In 2012, Portland State University (PSU) launched *The Provost's Challenge*, a unique campus-wide design initiative and innovation competition that encouraged collaboration, community engagement, and crowdsourcing. Faculty and staff proposed projects, created teams, and consolidated ideas and proposals through both online and in-person public interactions. The effort engaged over 1,000 PSU employees, generated 162 proposals, and eventually resulted in 24 different projects winning funding. Among these wide-ranging projects were online degree and certificate programmes, hybrid campus/online courses, coaching for struggling students, and improvements to orientation and advising models. *The Provost's Challenge* identified barriers to student success, created community-driven solutions, and built systems in a disruptive, competitive environment.

This innovation effort grew into the ongoing *reTHINK PSU*, a campus-wide presidential initiative to deliver an education that serves more students with better outcomes while containing costs through curricular innovation, community engagement, and effective use of technology. PSU's mantra is 'Let Knowledge Serve the City', and the institution continues to focus on strategic project implementation as part of *reTHINK PSU*, and to embrace the innovation and change necessary to better serve students in higher education today.

'Three key components of leadership are vision, commitment, and participation. If you want a change, you have to get a champion for it.'

– *Wim Wiewel*

WIM WIEWEL
President of Portland State University
Years of Service: 2008-2017

Wim Wiewel holds degrees in sociology and urban planning from the University of Amsterdam in the Netherlands and a Ph.D. in sociology from Northwestern University. Wiewel was the eighth president of Portland State University from 2008 to 2017. He currently serves as the President of Lewis and Clark College in Portland, Oregon.

Under Wiewel's leadership, PSU developed five guiding themes: provide civic leadership through partnerships, improve student success, achieve global excellence, enhance educational opportunity, and expand resources and improve effectiveness. Under his tenure, PSU became the largest and most diverse university in the state. Retention and graduation rates increased every year, while funded research went up 50 percent, and fundraising tripled. His leadership earned him a 2014 CASE (Council for Advancement and Support of Education) Chief Executive Leadership Award.

Interview with

WIM WIEWEL

This Interview Has Been Edited and Condensed for Clarity

How has your personal journey informed your motivations to do this work?

I have always been a leader, starting in elementary school. I was always the class president (or wanting to be the class president) or the organizer of the event.

Growing up in the Netherlands, you are aware of big infrastructure works. That's why the Netherlands even exists—because they build dykes and polders to keep the water out. I was intrigued by national highway plans, fascinated with the urban environment, so I studied sociology but with an interest in urban sociology. It was more or less random that I got a job in Chicago at the Department of Urban Planning. When the director of the center left, I became acting director. Right around that time, I got my PhD, and when they did a search to fill that position on a permanent basis, with that came the faculty position in Urban Planning. So in a sense, I'm an accidental professor of urban planning.

It's not accidental that I'm a professor. I certainly applied to jobs like *community organizer* or *social service provider*. I was interested in doing good in some way in the city, but I also realized I wasn't really a frontline person. I was willing to be in the trenches part of the time, but I also wanted to be able to step back and reflect on, and write on, and possibly teach about what I was doing. The academy, of course, is a perfect place for that.

To pursue a PhD, you have to be willing to spend a lot of hours by yourself, so it attracts personalities who are not necessarily good about being with other folks. If you are just slightly better than most, you're going to fall up. That's how I describe my career. I didn't set out to become a president or dean or anything like that. But I benefited along the way from mentors who told me I had leadership potential and encouraged me to pursue things. I benefited from a whole variety of training programmes: the Committee on Institutional Cooperation (CIC) when I was in Chicago, a training programme at Wharton, a programme at Harvard…. So I've done various forms of leadership training, and those have been relevant and helpful.

What does *innovation* mean to you in the context of your work as an institutional leader?

I don't use the word *innovation* all that often. *Change, improvement, progress*, yes. *Innovation* always seems a little bit pretentious, frankly. I assume they mean a more drastic form of change than the gradual evolutionary process that always happens in organizations.

At Portland State, I would use the word *innovation* with regard to totally changing the nature of how we do our internal budgeting, or developing the performance-based budgeting that allows us to allocate cost. The other big one is *reTHINK PSU*, to really change and rethink how we went about our pedagogy.

How did you experience the severity of external pressures on your institution?

Portland State's community engagement came out of fights with our larger sister institutions that didn't want us to grow. That required us to create strong coalitions with the local business, government, political, and not-for-profit sections, because we needed them to stand up and say, 'Yes, we care about this university'. We attracted more and more faculty who saw their work as being about community engagement, and then it became self-propelling because now the whole faculty body was going that way.

I was influenced at that time by the rise of MOOCS [massive open online courses]. I didn't think it was necessarily the answer, but I did think that we couldn't keep doings things the way we always had. We were not going to be a MOOC university, but we needed to think about the availability of online learning and the new learning styles of people who are technological natives—how that changes what we do, how we do it, and who we do it for. It wasn't like all of a sudden half our students were signing up for MOOCS, but it was a big change in the environment that could become a crisis if we didn't deal with it. It would involve a focus on how to use technology to change the nature of our teaching.

How would you describe the leadership structure you created?

My three key components of leadership are vision, commitment, and participation. If you want a change, you have to get a champion for it. That person is, in a way, more important than the unit. There's got to be somebody whose responsibility is to really drive it. On the whole, that is how you're most likely to be successful. The risk of that model is that if you make it a unit, that unit ends up being vulnerable if there's a leadership change.

Clearly, there is a team. We've spent a lot of time doing team-building exercises over the years with retreats and with different compositions of the executive committee. But I'd be lying if I didn't admit that I've played a pretty big role in issues. Certainly, other members of the executive committee have brought issues to the floor. The performance-based budgeting, the initiative for that did come from me, but 90 percent of the actual making it happen came from the Vice President of Finance and Administration, first, and then to some extent the provost as well.

If you talk about the general leadership model, it's certainly a system of distributed power. It's not like every decision either runs through me or even through the executive committee. There's a lot of power vested in the deans when it comes to the colleges, in the vice presidents for their divisions, in the various unit directors for their units. It's an organization where power is fairly decentralized. I don't want to say it's democratic or bottom-up, but units have a fair amount of autonomy over their activities.

How did you frame your vision for this work? What was the story you told about why this was important?

A vision does not arise full-blown from the leader's head, but it comes from the leader's interpretation of the institution and where it wants to go. But you can't

Chapter 8: **Portland State University**

do it without participation. It's got to be based on broad participation.

One of the most important roles of a leader is to be the "storyteller-in-chief". You allow people to see the best in a new light. There's a story about three baseball umpires discussing how they call balls and strikes. The first one says, 'I call 'em as I see em'. The second one says, 'I call 'em as they are". The third one says, 'They ain't anything until I call them'. It's the notion of respective sense-making. You tell the story of where the institution has been, the challenges it has faced, how it came to be where it is now. Obviously it has to be grounded in truth, but all stories are selections. All histories are selections that become compelling stories to help people understand why we are where we are now–and how they might move forward, building on that history, facing those challenges, or taking advantage of those historic opportunities.

Portland State University Visual Case Study

Sense-Making

The reallocation inspired *The Provost's Challenge*, a campus-wide design initiative to fund innovative faculty and staff projects and student-experience improvement grants. Leaders of *The Provost's Challenge* decided to use crowdsourcing and had to improvise the design, methodology, and the technology to launch the initiative. The barrier to entry was low: Proposals required only a title, a paragraph describing the project, and more than one author. They received 162 proposals.

Spark

In response to environmental and funding pressures, PSU closed its extended studies programme, which included siloed programmes for online classes, executive education programmes, and summer school. Administration received permission from the student body to reallocate $4 million budgeted for online course development towards an "innovation initiative" to improve the student experience.

New Vision

While *The Provost's Challenge* provided a platform and money for important projects and innovations in the university, its larger impact was the beginning of a sea change in how the university approached innovation through co-creation, crowdsourcing, and "design-thinking" methodologies centering the student experience.

Executive Leadership

President Wiewel hired Provost Sona Andrews to address the emerging challenges facing the university and to serve as a champion for the change effort. Andrews was less concerned with defining the future organization; her leadership process was to ask critical questions, then provide a forum and process for the university community to develop solutions. She developed cross-disciplinary teams that were given authority and autonomy and the responsibility to take risks to drive innovation.

Team/Mandate

The success of *The Provost's Challenge* eventually led to the creation of the Office of Academic Innovation to support innovations across the organization, such as *reTHINK PSU* and the advising redesign.

Iteration

Crowdsourcing and design thinking has engaged students, staff, and faculty in creating a culture that supports innovation and change.

Portland State University
reTHINK PSU

PROVOST'S CHALLENGE

The Provost's Challenge defined specific problems and solutions by funding small innovations across the university:

- **The Acceleration Challenge:** Innovations for online programmes and degrees that addressed student success, time-to-degree, and cost

- **Reframing Challenge:** Innovations leveraging technology to reimagine credit assignment, proficiency development, credentialing, and collaboration—both within and without the Oregon University System—to increase completion rates

- **Inspiration Challenge:** Low-cost, technology-based solutions to improve student success and graduation rates

reTHINK PSU

A campus-wide effort was initiated to deliver student services with better outcomes and contain costs through innovation, resulting in the following initiatives:

- **Flexible Degrees Programme:** Leveraging experiments from *The Provost's Challenge*, this programme was built from innovative experimentation (rather than traditional strategic planning) to provide flexible learning for non-traditional students.

- **Student Success Initiative:** Focused on removing barriers to student success and graduation, leaders followed a "design-thinking" methodology to center the student experience in their research. Among the projects developed were redesigned advising programmes, a new academic home for undeclared students, a coordinated service network, data-driven student interventions, and online portals for academic coaching, career services, and tutoring

Who They Serve

Portland State University is Oregon's most diverse public research university and the only urban public university in the state.

Providing Access

PSU's admission criteria for college freshman is a minimum 3.0 GPA or a combination of GPA and SAT/ACT scores. PSU also partners with state community colleges to provide access to returning adult learners and students not meeting freshman acceptance criteria.

Enabling Success

Many of the recent programmatic innovations at PSU involve reducing barriers for student success, including flexible degrees for returning adult students, redesigned advising programmes, streamlined administrative processes, and degree maps to support course selection.

THIS BOOK NEED NOT END HERE...

Share

All our books—including the one you have just read—are free to access online so that students, researchers and members of the public who can't afford a printed edition will have access to the same ideas. This title will be accessed online by hundreds of readers each month across the globe: why not share the link so that someone you know is one of them?

This book and additional content is available at:
https://doi.org/10.11647/OBP.0157

Customise

Personalise your copy of this book or design new books using OBP and third-party material. Take chapters or whole books from our published list and make a special edition, a new anthology or an illuminating coursepack. Each customised edition will be produced as a paperback and a downloadable PDF.

Find out more at:
https://www.openbookpublishers.com/section/59/1

Like Open Book Publishers

Follow @OpenBookPublish

Read more at the Open Book Publishers BLOG

YOU MAY ALSO BE INTERESTED IN:

OPEN EDUCATION
International Perspectives in Higher Education

Patrick Blessinger and TJ Bliss (eds.)

https://doi.org/10.11647/OBP.0103

DIGITAL HUMANITIES PEDAGOGY
Practices, Principles and Politics

Brett D. Hirsch (ed.)

https://doi.org/10.11647/OBP.0024

SOCIAL MEDIA AND HIGHER EDUCATION
Case Studies, Reflections and Analysis

Chris Rowell (ed.)

https://doi.org/10.11647/OBP.0162

www.ingramcontent.com/pod-product-compliance
Lightning Source LLC
Chambersburg PA
CBHW051551220426
43671CB00025B/3000

9 781783 745951